Alexander Thom und Co.

Commissioners of Public Works Ireland

Sixty-seventh report with appendices

Alexander Thom und Co.

Commissioners of Public Works Ireland
Sixty-seventh report with appendices

ISBN/EAN: 9783742804150

Manufactured in Europe, USA, Canada, Australia, Japa

Cover: Foto ©ninafisch / pixelio.de

Manufactured and distributed by brebook publishing software
(www.brebook.com)

Alexander Thom und Co.

Commissioners of Public Works Ireland

PUBLIC WORKS, IRELAND.

SIXTY-SEVENTH ANNUAL REPORT

OF THE

COMMISSIONERS OF PUBLIC WORKS

IN

IRELAND:

WITH

APPENDICES,

FOR THE YEAR ENDING 31ST MARCH, 1899.

Presented to Parliament by Command of Her Majesty.

DUBLIN:
PRINTED FOR HER MAJESTY'S STATIONERY OFFICE,
BY ALEXANDER THOM & CO. (LIMITED).

And to be purchased, either directly or through any Bookseller, from
Hodges, Figgis, and Co. (Limited), 104, Grafton-street, Dublin; or
Eyre and Spottiswoode, East Harding-street, Fleet-street, E.C., and
32, Abingdon-street, Westminster, S.W.; or
John Menzies and Co., 12, Hanover-street, Edinburgh, and 90, West Nile-street, Glasgow.

1899.

TABLE OF CONTENTS.

REPORT AND APPENDICES.

PUBLIC WORKS, IRELAND.

SIXTY-SEVENTH ANNUAL REPORT

OF THE

COMMISSIONERS OF PUBLIC WORKS IN IRELAND,

FOR THE YEAR 1898-99.

TO THE LORDS COMMISSIONERS OF HER MAJESTY'S TREASURY.

MAY IT PLEASE YOUR LORDSHIPS,

WE beg to submit the Sixty-seventh Annual Report of the Board.

We proceed to deal with the transactions of the year 1898-9 in the order adopted in the reports of late years :—

(1.) Voted Services, i.e., services for which provision is made by votes of Parliament.

(2.) Light Railways and Tramways.

(3.) Non-voted Services, i.e., services provided for from sources other than Parliamentary votes.

(4.) Loans.

Our Report, like that of last year, consists of statements and observations on matters under each of the four divisions just set forth which appear to deserve special notice. Details as to the various services are given in the Appendices.

The votes for "Public Works and Buildings" and "Public Works Office," may be regarded as the normal and permanent Parliamentary provisions administered by the Board. The vote for Railways (Ireland) appeared for the first time after the passing of the Light Railways and Tramways Act of 1883, and was continued by the operation of the Light Railways Act of 1889, and certain other statutes. The sums allocated by Parliament under these statutes are now virtually exhausted. The Light Railways Act of 1896, which provided £500,000 for expenditure on Railways, Steamboat, and Coach Services, and certain purposes in aid of those services, is at present in course of administration.

I.—VOTED SERVICES.

This head comprises the services created by, or maintained from, annual votes of Parliament. The following Table shows the expenditure for the last and two preceding years :—

—	1898-99.	1897-98.	1896-97.
	£	£	£
Class I.—Public Works and Buildings, Ireland,	202,430	207,863	211,965
Do., Railways, Ireland,	91,874	89,970	96,635
Class II.—Public Works Office,	39,365	38,993	39,017
£	333,659	331,736	319,617

Details of the provision made by Parliament for the year 1898-99 for Public Works and Buildings will be found at pp. 58-65 of the Estimates for that year; for Railways at pp. 66-67; and for Public Works Office at pp. 190-192.

The Voted services Class 1 comprise—

Public Buildings, Ireland, viz. :—

Naval and Military; State and Official Residences; Civil Departments; Legal Departments; Metropolitan Police; Royal Irish Constabulary; Dundrum Criminal Lunatic Asylum, Science and Art Department; Public Education; Royal University and Queen's Colleges; Revenue Departments.

Royal Parks and Gardens :—

Phoenix Park; St. Stephen's-green; The Curragh of Kildare.

Royal Harbours :—

Kingstown, Howth; Donaghadee; Dunmore; Ardglass.

Inland Navigation :—

Malgue.

Ancient Monuments Protection Act, 1882, 45 & 46 Vic., c. 73.
Ditto, ditto, 1892, 55 & 56 Vic., c. 46.

Tramways and Light Railways—See also pages 10 to 15.

National School Grants.

During the year the commencement of works was authorised at 178 schools; issues at foot of grants were made to 194; and 72 new schools, the building of which was aided by grant, were completed. Amongst the last were the following important schools: Castleisland Convent School; Crumlin-road, Belfast; St. Patrick's, Bray; St. Columba's, Clontarf; St. Stephen's, Waterford.

A sum of £33,500 was provided by the estimates for 1898-99 to meet the demands for grants during the year. The expenditure reached only £27,131, and thus £6,369 was left unspent out of the provision, and returned to the Exchequer. Every effort was made to lead Managers of schools to push on the works aided by grant as quickly as possible, in order to enable the full amount provided to be utilised. The Board issued letters to Managers in cases where progress of building was slow, urging them to expedition, and the Local Officers of the Department, under special instructions, impressed on them the importance of avoiding delay. In addition, the Board put themselves in communication with the Commissioners of National Education on the subject, and the Departments co-operated in the endeavour to secure full expenditure. Had these courses not been adopted, the expenditure would, in all probability, have fallen short of the £27,131 actually expended.

Our Report for 1895-96 (p. 8) referred to certain changes in the regulations of the Commissioners of National Education, which had been adopted after consultation with this Board for the purpose of securing that, when grants have been sanctioned, expenditure should not be unduly postponed by delay on the part of Managers to commence or complete building. It pointed out that the delays on the part of Managers had been shown by experience to lead in many years to the partial non-expenditure of the sum voted by Parliament for grants, and to hamper both Departments in dealing with new applications for aid by grant.

Several of the conditions to which grants are subject are aimed at securing the early commencement and steady prosecution of work, so as to secure full expenditure of the provision for grants. Thus, the Commissioners of National Education require that in case the local contribution is in cash, the money, or a due proportion of it, shall be already available; that if it takes the form of labour and assistance in providing materials, it shall be available without delay; that the works shall be commenced within three months from the date upon which commencement shall be authorised; and that they shall be completed within eighteen months from the date of authorisation. These conditions, aided by reminders from the two Departments, secured full expenditure in 1895-96 and 1896-97. They have not been successful for the two following years. The difficulty experienced by Managers in carrying on building operations in remote rural districts, with inexperienced contractors, or without a contractor, is no doubt a principal cause of delay, and one with which it is not easy to cope.

The following table shows the amounts voted and expended on Grants since 1879–80, when the system was introduced.

Year.	Provision.	Expenditure.
	£	£
1879–80,	5,000	10,512
1880–81,	8,000	8,466
1881–82,	10,000	10,246
1882–83,	10,000	9,604
1883–84,	10,000	17,451
1884–85,	11,160	22,912
1885–86,	25,000	29,134
1886–87,	30,000	41,250
1887–88,	46,000	51,623
1888–89,	40,000	41,495
1889–90,	40,000	31,100
1890–91,	40,000	37,231
1891–92,	40,000	30,014
1892–93,	30,000	24,283
1893–94,	30,000	23,196
1894–95,	25,000	30,179
1895–96,	40,000	40,000
1896–97,	40,000	40,000
1897–98,	40,000	38,600
1898–99,	52,500	57,131

Postal Stores, Aldborough House, Dublin.

The alterations and additions to this building, the programme of which was set forth in our Report for 1897-98, pp. 7 and 8, have been completed, and the Stationery, Clothing, and other Postal Stores transferred to it, together with the clerical staff of the Stores Branch. In addition, the building provides full accommodation for the three Postal Surveyors for Ireland and their respective staffs, and for the Superintending Telegraph Engineer and his staff. The stores transferred include those connected with the Telegraph Service, and workshops for mechanics in the employ of the Post Office are also provided on the premises. Aldborough House now makes a suitable central depot for all the general stores of the Post Office Department for Ireland, from which distribution to the various localities can be made. There is also available considerable space for the Christmas pressure of the Parcel Post Department, the principal office of which is situated at no great distance, and it was used for that purpose with satisfactory results in December, 1898.

The entire cost of the adaptation has been £7,457 14s. 2d.

Belfast Parcels Post Depot and Telegraph Engineer's Workshops.

This building was practically completed in the year under report. It is connected with the older Postal buildings by a bridge across Charlemont-street. It was used, and its arrangements found satisfactory, in December last during the pressure of Christmas parcel business. In addition to the Parcels Receiving Department, there are large sorting and distributing rooms provided, with adequate accommodation for the clerical staff. The ground floor contains a Night Delivery Telegraph Office. Sound-proof Telephone rooms are provided on the upper floor. The building comprises also Telegraph stores and mechanics' workshops.

Dining accommodation is arranged on the second floor for the whole of the staff of the new, and also of the older buildings. Room has been found for the kitchen and its appurtenances without inconvenience to general purposes, and a kitchen yard on the level of the kitchen floor has been formed over the roof of a portion of the building which was not carried to the same height as the body of the offices.

Two sets of electric lights have been provided, and are worked by a current taken from the Corporation mains.

DUNDRUM CRIMINAL LUNATIC ASYLUM.

Early in the financial year, His Excellency the Lord Lieutenant caused inquiry to be made into proposals for improvements to the Dundrum Criminal Lunatic Asylum, additional to those which have been carried out during the last few years. The institution has hitherto been partially heated by open fires, and the laundry work has been carried on by hand labour. The desirability of an improved heating system had been previously felt, but it was not practicable to make the necessary arrangements until important structural alterations in the quarters occupied by the inmates, which had been in progress, were completed. The result of the investigations directed by the Lord Lieutenant was a decision to provide immediately heating, laundry machinery, and certain minor improvements in the cooking arrangements. These works will necessitate the erection of a boiler-house and certain structural changes in and additions to the existing laundry premises.

The choice of a heating system suitable to an existing, and especially a masonry, building is generally a restricted one. After consideration, it was determined to adopt low-pressure hot-water heating by steam injection, with radiators, ordinary and ventilating, in the principal rooms and passages, and pipes in other parts of the building. In the single rooms the pipes will be run on the ceilings, so as to keep them out of the patients' reach. The injection for the pipes and radiators will be effected by three Sirius Injectors, placed at well distributed positions in the building. There will be a maximum overflow from the summit of the system of about 180 gallons of hot water per hour, which will be utilised for feeding the boilers.

The new laundry arrangements will provide suitable receiving, washing, drying, and finishing rooms, with a new delivery room and foul wash-house. The new boiler-house will be capable of accommodating three boilers if necessary. For the present provision is being made of two Lancashire cross-tube boilers, 6 feet 6 inches in diameter, and 24 feet long. The chimney stack will be placed as far as practicable from the laundry and drying-ground.

Contracts were made for the machinery required for the purposes described in the year under report, and delivery made of portion of the orders. The work will be completed in the present year.

A portion of the boundary wall which required early restoration was rebuilt to an increased height.

QUEENSTOWN CUSTOM HOUSE.

This building has been completed and occupied. The front is built of red Ruabon brick, with suitable facings, and the work, taken with the works in course of erection by the local authorities in its vicinity, is an improvement to the appearance of the town. Of the two storeys comprising the Custom House, the ground floor provides on one side a boat-room, and on the other accommodation for Customs' business. The upper storey contains a large general office, with a smaller office for the Chief Officer, and some other accommodation.

In order to meet the views of the Town Commissioners, who have improved the roadway in front of the building so as to render it more suitable for vehicular traffic, the Board have had the flagstaff removed from the front to the rere, and a railing erected across the Custom House frontage on the quay wall.

NATIONAL LIBRARY, KILDARE-STREET.

The eastern wing of this building, though structurally complete as a part of the southern or main façade of the Library, had not, until the execution of the works about to be mentioned, been utilised or fitted up for any purpose. It contained two unfinished rooms, which have now been made available, one as a Refreshment Room, the other as an additional Reading Room. The Refreshment Room is on the ground floor, and is entered from the colonnade. It has been provided with durable fittings and furniture, in the selection of which regard has been had to the materials and style in which the fittings of the building generally have been carried out. Arrangements have been made, so far as necessary, for cooking purposes. The Refreshment Room is mainly intended, not only for the readers at the Library, but also for the students at the neighbouring School of Art and at the Science and Art Museum. It will also be available for officials and the public visiting the Science and Art Buildings. There had been no similar accommodation in the immediate neighbourhood of the buildings, and the want was much felt, and caused loss of time to students and readers.

The first floor contains the new Reading Room, which, it is understood, will be principally used by readers requiring to consult *éditions de luxe* and works and documents of special value demanding more than ordinary care. The appropriation of these two rooms disposes of all the accommodation actually available in the Library building as it stands.

Central Bridewell.

Provision was made in the Estimates for commencing this building, but owing to the difficulty in arranging for a suitable site, which was not obtained until the close of the year, progress was impracticable. The Central Bridewell system exists in Liverpool, Birmingham, Bristol, and other towns, its effect being to enable prolonged detention at outlying stations to be dispensed with, by which a more satisfactory treatment of prisoners and a certain economy in administration is secured.

The building, which will be of fireproof construction throughout, will comprise three storeys, with cells for 72 men and 48 women. The cells will be lighted from the outside, and will open off central corridors and galleries lighted from the top. It will also contain male and female receiving-rooms, a large day-room, children's rooms, bath-rooms, drying-rooms, lavatories, &c., as well as administrative accommodation, consisting of charge and escort rooms, Inspector's office, and various stores, &c.

The Bridewell will communicate with the Police Courts, adjacent to which it is to be built, by an underground passage.

II.—LIGHT RAILWAYS AND TRAMWAYS.

Railways (Ireland) Act, 1896, Coach and Steamer Services.

As mentioned in the Board's Annual Report for 1897–8, the grant of £9,500 to the Shannon Development Company was followed by the provision of an additional sum of £1,684 for expenditure by the Board on the repair and construction of certain piers in Lough Derg, and the cost of establishing a Coach Service between Rooskey and Dromod.

The works referred to were completed before the Steamer Service for the tourist season came into operation on 1st June, 1898.

The items composing them are stated in detail under the title of Non-Voted Services at p. 19.

Railways (Ireland) Act, 1896, Shannon Steamer Services.

The summer services came into operation on the 1st June and were continued until 30th September. They consisted of daily services between Killaloe and Athlone, and Athlone and Carrick-on-Shannon, and a cross service on Lough Derg. In October the modified winter services which had been approved by the Board in December, 1897, took the place of the summer arrangements. They provided:—

A bi-weekly service between Athlone and Killaloe;
A weekly service between Athlone and Rooskey;
A cross service on Lough Derg four times a week.

After an experience of three months of the winter services, it was shown by the Company that the receipts from the Athlone and Killaloe service were very small, and that the expense of maintaining a bi-weekly service was, under the circumstances, an undue tax on their resources.

It was further shown that the local service on Lough Derg had been so little used during the period stated that the revenue did not to any appreciable extent meet the expenses of the extra steamer which this service necessitated. The Company, under these circumstances, requested the Board to sanction a modification of the through services and the suspension of the cross service for the remainder of the winter and spring season.

The Board, in view of the statement submitted, approved of a modification of the Athlone and Killaloe service from a bi-weekly to a weekly, and a modification of the cross service on Lough Derg from four days a week to weekly. At the same time they required this last-mentioned service to be taken over an extended route, the boat to leave Killaloe and return thereto after having called at Mountshannon, Dromineer, and Williamstown, and that the mileage saved by these reductions in the winter service should be made up for by increased mileage during the tourist season.

The Athlone and Carrick-on-Shannon service was continued as a weekly service.

Site for Hotel at Killaloe, &c.

We have placed at the disposal of the Shannon Development Company (Limited) a site (containing 5a. 2r. 2p.) for a hotel on the east bank of the river at a short distance from the Waterford, Limerick and Western Railway Company's Terminus at Killaloe. The agreement on the subject contains provisions binding the Company to build a suitable hotel within a specified period. A sum of £800 has been paid by the Company for the site. We have also leased at Athlone a site (containing one-third of an acre) to the Company for a boatslip and workshop required for the maintenance and repair of the Company's fleet.

A site at Tarmonbarry has been leased to the Shannon Development Company at a nominal rent for a ticket office, and, finally, one, also at a nominal rent—for a ticket office at Killaloe.

Coach Service between Rooskey and Dromod.

The Lord Lieutenant's Certificate for this service was issued in April, 1898, and a contract for the working of the Coach each week-day between Rooskey Lock and Dromod Railway Station was arranged in the following month. The service establishes a connection between the trains of the Cavan and Leitrim Railway at Dromod and the Shannon Steamers at Rooskey. It came into operation on the 1st June, 1898. From the end of September the Coach ceased to run daily and a service sufficient to meet the reduced Steamer Service on the Shannon was substituted.

(2.)—Coach Service between Tarbert and Listowel.

This service, which was put into operation on the 1st June, 1897, has continued to be worked as a week-day service by the Development Syndicate, under a contract made with the Board on 14th February, 1898. It has proved an important connecting link between the Southern Railway systems and the West and North *via* Kilrush, Kilkee, and Ennis. During the last tourist season it was largely used by through passengers, the number of whom, as compared with the previous season, showed an appreciable increase.

In July last a waiting shed for passengers, containing also an office for the use of the Board's Agent, was erected at Tarbert Pier by the Contractors for the working of the Coach Service, in accordance with their agreement with the Board.

(3.)—Steamer Service on the Lower Shannon between Tarbert, County Kerry, and Kilrush, County Clare.

This service, as provided by the agreement made by the Board with the Contractors, the Waterford Steamship Company, is worked on each week-day during the Summer months from 1st June to 30th September. It came into operation on the 1st June, 1897. It worked satisfactorily during the Summer season of 1898, the number of passengers being considerably in excess of the previous season. It connects with the Tarbert and Listowel Coach at Tarbert, and with the trains of the West and South Clare Railways at Cappa Pier, Kilrush.

An effort was made to enable the steamer which carries out the Board's service to be utilised for the purpose of plying between Tarbert and Foynes, so as to permit visitors to Kilkee to travel by rail (Waterford and Limerick Company) from Limerick to Foynes, and by steamer from Foynes to Kilrush *via* Tarbert, completing the journey to

Kilkee by the South Clare Line, and vice versa. The Board offered every practicable facility for the purpose indicated, but the Waterford and Limerick Railway Company did not for the time being see their way to make the arrangements as to arrival and departure of trains required in connection with the proposal.

(4.)—Coach Service between Ennistymon and Ballyvaughan, via Lisdoonvarna.

This service, which plies on alternate week-days during the Summer months (June to September, inclusive) showed during the late season an increase in number of passengers as compared with 1897. A tidal steamer service, worked by a company, connects Ballyvaughan with the town of Galway.

Sligo and Belmullet Steamer Service.

An agreement was negotiated in the year under report, and has been entered into since its completion, with the Sligo Steam Navigation Company for the working of a Steamer Service between Sligo and Belmullet for a term of seven years, power being reserved to the Board to determine the agreement at any time after the expiration of the first two years on six months notice. The Company have purchased a suitable steamer (the *Tartar*) found for that purpose by the Board, who take a mortgage on the vessel to secure themselves in certain events in respect of the purchase money, and the cost of alterations required to fit her for the service. The Board will pay the Company an inclusive sum of £4,230 per annum for the working of the service. The receipts are to be collected and paid to the Board.

The sailings will be tri-weekly in each direction from the 1st May to the 30th September, and bi-weekly in each direction for the remainder of the year, with such variations as in the opinion of the Board circumstances may require, from time to time. The steamer will serve passenger and goods traffic at intermediate points as circumstances permit.

It was originally contemplated by the Irish Government to establish a steamer service between Achill Sound and Belmullet, with a pier at Gubbardletter, Achill, and to establish connection by a short railway between that pier and the Achill Station of the Midland Great Western Railway Company. These arrangements were sanctioned by certificates of the Lord Lieutenant under Sec. 9 of the Railways (Ireland) Act, of 1896, dated 2nd November, 1896, and 16th May, 1897. This scheme was abandoned under the circumstances detailed in our Report for 1897-98, p. 13.

The Irish Government then substituted the service between Sligo and Belmullet, and the certificate covering the latter service was issued by His Excellency, on 7th December, 1897.

The new pier at Broadhaven Bay, on the north side of the town of Belmullet, required for the purposes of this service, and referred to in p. 18 of our Report for 1897-98, is in course of erection. After careful examination a site was chosen at Pickle Point, about one mile from the town. Plans and specifications were prepared, and tenders for construction having been invited by advertisement in October last, ten were received. That of Mr. J. Hemingway, of Belfast, was accepted, and the construction was begun in due course. The structure will consist of a timber pier with a store and other works suitable for the working of the service. The main pier head is to be sixty-five feet long over the outside of the pile heads, and is to consist of nine frames of three piles each. A railing four feet high is to extend along a portion of the back of the pier head and along both sides of the gangway, which is to be carried on thirty-three frames of two piles each.

A tramway is to be laid along the gangway on the top of the decking, and a truck supplied for the purpose of carrying, &c., between the steamer and a store. The latter (size thirty feet by sixteen feet) will be erected at the shore end of the pier, and a portion of it will be partitioned off and fitted up as an Agent's Office. The contract price of the work is £3,364.

Communication between Belmullet and the district south of that town will also be facilitated, as the amount set apart for pier construction includes the cost of a new pier at Blacksod Bay, which it is proposed to erect at the south end of the road, lately constructed, leading to the town.

Legal Effect of Awards under Tramway and Public Companies (Ireland) Act, 1883.

This Act gave Counties power to guarantee the dividends on capital subscribed for the construction of Railways under it, and created a system of arbitration for the purpose of ascertaining the amount to be paid under such guarantees. It further enabled the Treasury to undertake the recoupment of a proportion of the amount paid by a guaranteeing county in aid of dividends. The Act made the awards of the Arbitrators binding on the Counties and Baronies. It was inevitable that questions should arise as to the correctness of the awards, and that such questions should raise the further question, whether the Treasury was at liberty to contest the awards. When this last-mentioned point presented itself, it became necessary to place it in train for legal decision, in order to avoid the risk of misappropriation of moneys voted by Parliament.

The question presented itself definitely in the circumstances which led to the case of Kelly *versus* the Queen, which was decided in the year under report by the Queen's Bench Division of the High Court of Justice in Ireland, in the first instance, and subsequently by the Court of Appeal. It arose in connection with the Athenry and Tuam (Extension to Claremorris) Railway, the dividends of which were guaranteed by the County of Mayo, under the Act of 1883. The accounts dealt with by the Arbitrator's Award for the half-year ending 31st October, 1895, included in the charges of the half-year expenditure made previous to that period, part of which was made before the regular opening of the line for traffic. The Board were advised that this expenditure was incorrectly included, and that the Treasury were not bound by the Award. Under these circumstances, it became necessary that the matter should be made the subject of judicial decision, and payment of the sum in dispute having been withheld with that object, a Petition of Right was brought by a ratepayer against the Crown. The Supreme Court held in favour of this petition, and the Court of Appeal confirmed this decision. The Treasury thereupon caused the full amount claimed under the Award to be paid.

While the question whether the Crown was bound by the awards was undecided the Board, acting under legal advice, abstained from appearing before the Arbitrators. They are now free to take part in the proceedings, and, with your Lordships' sanction, have done so in more than one case since the close of the year.

West and South Clare Railways Working Agreement, &c.

The Board found it necessary to intervene before the Board of Trade, with reference to an agreement between the West Clare and South Clare Company, for the working of the South Clare line, under the following circumstances.

Both lines were constructed under the Act of 1883. Dividends on their capitals are guaranteed by the County, and the Treasury have undertaken liability for partial recoupment of sums paid in aid of guaranteed dividend. Your Lordships have, therefore, an interest in seeing that expenditure on the working and management of the lines is made on the principles laid down by the Order in Council and Acts governing them.

The South Clare Line has been worked since its opening by the West Clare Company under agreements binding for a year, a new agreement being thus required annually. Up to the close of 1898 the agreements made no provision for any charge against the South Clare Company for the use of the West Clare Rolling Stock, or for the use of the joint station at Miltown Malbay. In the course of 1898 the propriety of making such provision was discussed between the Companies and the Board of Works, and the agreement prepared and adopted by the Companies for 1899 recognised it in principle, imposing on the South Clare Company an annual charge of £100 for the use of the West Clare Rolling Stock, and an annual rent of £25 for the use of the Miltown Malbay Station. The Board regarded these charges on the South Clare Company as inadequate. The agreement, as prepared, apportioned between the lines by lineal mileage certain items of expenditure which, it appeared to the Board, should have been apportioned by train mileage. The points just mentioned, with certain others, were brought by the Board under the consideration of the Board of Trade. What necessitated this step was that the undercharging of the South Clare Line and the overcharging of the West Clare Line in the past had unduly increased the Baronial contribution to the dividend of the West Clare Line, and had thus also increased the Treasury liability for recoupment in respect of that Line. If the South Clare Line had borne its fair share of working expenses, the Treasury contribution in respect of the West Clare Line would have been diminished without entailing on every occasion a corresponding increase in the case of the South Clare Line. This results from the fact that the South Clare Line does not always pay its working expenses; that when it fails to do so the entire dividend, together with any deficit on working, has to be provided by the contributing area, and that in such a state of things the Treasury liability for recoupment necessarily reaches the maximum under the Act of 1883, which cannot be exceeded, no matter how heavy the working expenses have been.

The Board of Trade increased considerably the charge for rolling stock, confirmed the agreement as to the mode of charge by mileage, and altered the provision of a fixed sum for the use of the joint station to an arrangement that the cost of working it should be divided between the two lines in the proportions of their respective traffics.

It is anticipated that such questions as led to the application to the Board of Trade will, if they arise, become more easy of arrangement in the future. The Board is being brought into closer relations with the Companies formed under the Act of 1883 by the systematic examination of their accounts with a view to taking part in the proceedings before the Arbitrators. These examinations will give opportunity for the friendly discussion of points of difference, if any present themselves.

As the result of an investigation of the accounts of the West and South Clare Companies for the half-year ending 31st October, 1897, made in 1898, consideration was directed to the difference between the lines in cost of working, that of the South Clare for the half-year, being 1s. 10½d. per train mile, as compared with 3s. 1½d. for the West Clare. Attention was also given to certain items, particularly to a large sum charged against the West Clare line for purchase of materials in the half-year. It appeared that only a comparatively small part of these materials was used during the period, and there was also a question as to whether some portion of the amount charged for these against the West Clare Company should not have been added to the charge for materials against the South Clare.

In January, 1899, the accounts of the West and South Clare Companies for the half-year ending 31st October, 1898, were examined by an official of the Board, acting by Treasury authority. The result was that certain items of expenditure appeared to the Board to require special consideration at the coming Arbitration.

The meeting of the Arbitrators, at which the Board was represented, was held on the 31st January. The more salient matters above mentioned relating to the accounts for the half-year ending 31st October, 1897, came under notice with the accounts for the October 1898 half year. The Arbitrators made a reduction of £666 in the case of the West Clare line as regards the sums chargeable against the half-year. Of the entire reduction, £333 was in relief of the Baronies and a similar amount in relief of the Treasury. In the case of the South Clare line, they made a reduction of £261 for the half-year, of which £195 was in relief of the Baronies and £66 in relief of the Treasury, making a total reduction for the particular half-year in relief of the Baronies of £528, and in relief of the Treasury £399, or an aggregate reduction of £927.

It will be seen that the question before the Arbitrators was mainly whether the expense incurred in purchase of materials was chargeable in the accounts of the half-year in question. The materials in respect of which the adjustment of overcharge was made will be used in due course, and their cost will be duly charged, as consumption progresses, against each of the lines.

The Company had proposed to place the sum representing the overcharge to a suspense account. The Arbitrators declined to approve of this course and included the amount in the aggregate of reduction of £927 already mentioned.

In December, 1897, the Irish Government referred to the Board a Memorial numerously signed by ratepayers and others interested in these Railways, complaining of unsatisfactory management in several important respects. After communication with the West Clare Company, we appointed an experienced railway officer to hold an inquiry under Section 7 of the Railways (Ireland) Act, 1896. The Investigator, accompanied by an officer of the Board, when on his way to Kilrush, where the inquiry was to be held, learned at Limerick from several persons who had signed the Memorial that they had done so without particular inquiry into the specific statements made in it, and that they should not be taken as endorsing those statements. The inquiry showed that while there were imperfections in the administration of the line, and while certain matters required adjustment, there was no substantial foundation for a large number of the statements contained in the Memorial. We were of opinion, that on the whole, the circumstances did not warrant a recommendation to His Excellency the Lord Lieutenant to exercise the power given him by the section alluded to of appointing a Manager or Receiver. We communicated with the West Clare Company as to the matters which required adjustment and improvement.

Donegal and Killybegs Railway; Stranorlar and Glenties Railway.

In 1897 it was considered that an investigation of the accounts of these lines was desirable, and a railway expert was employed, and reported on several matters which appeared to require adjustment. We then brought the points referred to under the notice of the working company (Donegal Railway Company), and it was agreed in the main that our contentions were correct, and that certain receipts should be apportioned and certain charges should be made on the bases we contended for. Some points remained which it was agreed to refer to arbitration. By common consent, Mr. Seady, formerly Secretary to this Board, and also Arbitrator appointed by the Board of Trade under the Tramways (Ireland) Act, 1883, was named to settle the items still in dispute, and to adjust the book accounts on the basis of the decisions already accepted by the Company and of his settlement of the disputed points.

The result of Mr. Seady's arbitration on accounts up to November, 1897, was an award that the county (Donegal) and Treasury were entitled to receive from the Company the following sums:—

(1.) Donegal and Killybegs Railway:—The Treasury to receive £245 9s. 4d.; the county to receive £636 17s. 4d.

(2.) Stranorlar and Glenties Railway:—The Treasury to receive £101 7s. 1d.; the county to receive £5.

Mr. Seady, however, reserved certain points for the decision of a court of law; they were briefly as follows:—

(1.) Whether the Donegal and Killybegs Railway was properly chargeable with any sum for the use of Donegal Station, and as a contribution towards the rent of £200 a year paid by the Donegal Railway Company for the station.

(2.) Whether the Stranorlar and Glenties Line was properly chargeable with any payments to the Donegal Railway Company in respect of the use of the Stranorlar Station.

(3.) Whether it was competent for the Arbitrator to deal with the balance of £636 17s. 4d. declared to be payable to the county.

(4.) To whom or for what purpose the said balance should be paid.

The case was finally decided by the Court of Appeal on appeal from the Court of Queen's Bench:—

(1.) It was conceded by us that part of the rent of Donegal Station was chargeable to the Donegal and Killybegs Line.

(2.) It was decided that no rent was payable for Stranorlar Station.

(3.) and (4.) As regards the item of £636 17s. 4d., it was held that, as the county was no party to the arbitration, and as the award was therefore wanting in the element of mutuality, that the amount (£636 17s. 4d.) could not under the award be claimed for the county. The same principle applies to the sum declared payable to the county in respect of the Stranorlar and Glenties Line.

The effect of the decision on point (2) is to increase the amount awarded originally to the Treasury in the case of the Stranorlar and Glenties from £100 7s. 1d. to £169 14s. 4d.

The proceedings have settled important principles, from which considerable benefit will be derived in the future.

In connection with the financial investigation of 1897, an investigation was held under section 7 of the Railways (Ireland) Act, 1896, into the condition, working, &c., of these lines. The result was, on the whole, satisfactory, some minor points alone requiring attention.

CARNDONAGH AND BUNCRANA, AND LETTERKENNY AND BURTONPORT RAILWAYS.

In June, 1898, we proceeded to select an Engineer to represent the Board in connection with the railways to be constructed in Donegal County. Candidates with experience in the construction of lines through mountainous and sparsely populated districts were invited by advertisement, and a considerable number of applications were received. After consideration of qualifications and testimonials, an interview was held with Mr. J. H. Ryan, M.A., M.INST. C.E., of this city, who has had large experience in connection with railway engineering. As he was not prepared to take up a temporary post under the condition of devoting himself to it to the exclusion of private practice, we proceeded to make a selection from the general body of applicants. The range of choice was finally narrowed to two, who were subjected to a careful oral inquiry into their training, previous employment, and familiarity with the class of work to be done. Both candidates showed capacity and knowledge. One of them, Mr. T. M. Batchen, disclosed large recent experience in lines very similar to those to be undertaken. The other had been employed in connection with lines of a heavier construction. The former was appointed to the post, and has since rendered valuable service to the Board.

As stated in our last Annual Report, the amount of the lowest tender for the Carndonagh Line was much above the Investigator's estimate, and it became necessary to arrange for a reduced specification in order that satisfactory financial arrangements might be made for the work of construction. As an additional security for obtaining a satisfactory tender, it was decided that the line should be re-advertised at the same time as tenders should be invited for the Burtonport Railway. The Act of Parliament confirming the Order of the Privy Council for the construction, &c., of the latter line was passed on the 25th July, 1898, but, in anticipation of its passing, the detailed working plans and specification had been put in hands and were ready for printing off in August of 1898. They showed considerable economy as compared with the plans and specification for the Carndonagh Railway, and, as both lines were to be maintained and worked by the Lough Swilly Railway Company, the Board were desirous that the standard adopted in the plans and specification for the Burtonport Railway should be made applicable also to the Carndonagh Line. Prolonged negotiations with the Company followed with a view to this end, and in the outcome the Company agreed that reductions should be made in the general works of the line, effecting a considerable saving, without, however, reducing the standard of the line below the standard—viz. the Stranorlar and Glenties Railway—which had been agreed upon in 1897 between the Company and the Board as the standard for the Carndonagh Line. It was also agreed, in lieu of one inclusive contract for each line, covering all expenses, that the cost of land and the amounts allowed for engineering, legal, and promotion expenses should be defrayed directly by the Board of Works, and that contractors should be afforded an opportunity of tendering separately for the general works of the line, permanent way, and, in the case of the Burtonport Railway, stations, the stations for the Carndonagh Line being constructed under the revised agreement by the Company for a sum agreed upon.

Tenders were accordingly invited, and those of Messrs. Pauling & Co., Limited, Westminster, proved to be considerably the lowest, and upon the report of the Board on the tenders, Your Lordships were pleased, on the 23rd March last, to authorise the Board to accept Messrs. Paulings' tenders for the general works and permanent way of the Carndonagh Line and the Burtonport Line, and also for the stations of the latter line.

Without going into the details of the communications that thereupon passed between the Board and the Lough Swilly Railway Company, we may state that, on the 13th May, the Privy Council passed Orders extending the time for the construction of the two lines, and contracts were entered into with Messrs. Pauling & Co. in accordance with Your Lordships' authority. The first sod of the Carndonagh Line was cut by Lady Betty Balfour on Tuesday, the 23rd May, and the works are being actively prosecuted. The commencement of the work for the Burtonport Line has also been made at the Letterkenny end, and at the date of this Report preparations are being made for commencing it also at the Burtonport end.

III.—NON-VOTED SERVICES.

National and Ancient Monuments.

As the Local Government Act of 1898 gives County Councils powers, hereinafter specifically referred to, for the conservation of National and Ancient Monuments, it may be of interest to state the general conditions, legal and financial, under which that service has been conducted. As hereafter explained, "Ancient" Monuments are provided for in the Annual Estimates; but as "National" Monuments are provided for out of other sources, and as the latter are the class that was first placed under the Board, we deal with both groups under the head of Non-Voted Services.

The 25th Section of the Irish Church Act (32 and 33 Vic., c. 42) provided that where any church or ecclesiastical building appeared to the Commissioners of the Church Temporalities to be ruinous or (if a church) to be disused as a place of worship and not suitable for restoration for worship and yet deserving of being maintained as a National Monument, the Commissioners should by order vest such structure in the Board of Works to be preserved as a National Monument.

The Section further directed the Church Temporalities Commissioners to ascertain the sum necessary for maintaining the structures to be vested, and pay it to the Board of Works to be applied to the maintenance of the structures vested.

The Church Act provided for the vesting of ecclesiastical structures only. The Ancient Monuments Protection Act, 1882 (45 and 46 Vic., c. 73) empowers the owner of any monument to which the Act applies to place it under the guardianship of the Commissioners of Public Works, who are thereupon clothed with the responsibility for its maintenance out of moneys to be voted by Parliament. A schedule specifies a number of monuments to which the Act is made applicable, and power is given to add to the list. Injury to a monument to which the Act applies is made punishable by fine or imprisonment, but this provision is not enforceable against the owner unless the Board have been constituted guardians of the monument.

The scope of the Board's duty was further enlarged by the Ancient Monuments Protection Act of 1892 (55 & 56 Vic., c. 46), which provides that where the Board are of opinion that the preservation of any ancient or mediæval monument is a matter of public interest by reason of the historic, traditional, or artistic interest attached thereto, they may, at the request of the owner, consent to become the guardians thereof, and thereupon the Ancient Monuments Protection Act, 1882, shall apply to such monument. The annual provision made by Parliament for the purposes of the Act of 1882 then becomes applicable to their maintenance. The Act of 1892 contains a provision having an important bearing on the application of the moneys placed at the disposition of the Board by Section 25 of the Irish Church Act already referred to. It enacts that where any monument is entrusted to the guardianship of the Board of a character similar to that described in the section just mentioned, the Board shall be at liberty to apply the funds of the Irish Church Act to its maintenance. In practice ecclesiastical monuments brought under guardianship under the Act of 1892 are maintained out of the last-mentioned fund, while non-ecclesiastical monuments are maintained out of the Parliamentary provision.

A sum of £50,000 was transferred to the Board by the Church Temporalities Commissioners under the Irish Church Act, and invested in £49,901 5s. 7d. Government Stock. Large demands on the fund arose for a considerable time after the creation of the service in consequence of the urgent necessity for immediate works to ensure the preservation of many of the structures vested. The yearly income derived from the investment was quite inadequate to meet these demands, and it became necessary to raise money for expenditure by sale of stock. The interest on the unsold securities is sufficient to meet the annual outgoings of the service. It is necessary to exercise caution in expenditure in view of the fall in income which will result from the reduction of interest on Government Stock in 1900.

Ancient Crosses, Monasterboice; Tumulus, New Grange.

as "formatori," of special skill in such matters. During its progress representations were made to the Board that there was reason to fear injury to the sculptured work on the Cross, from the mode in which the process was being carried out.

The subject was taken up promptly, inspections were made by the Board and by the Director of the Museum, and additional steps taken to secure the Cross against risk. After the work had been completed, it was found that the removal of lichens had given to the carvings a sharpness of outline which they did not previously possess. This, however, will be remedied in process of time by fresh growth. Otherwise the Cross is substantially unaffected. Every precaution will be taken in similar cases to secure that the process of cleaning be carried out by means which cannot possibly affect the surface of the stone. Permission for castings cannot be given in any case without the fullest investigation. A body like the Science and Art Department, or a learned Society which undertakes the work for the public benefit, and employs specially skilled persons, is indeed under ordinary circumstances alone entitled to be entrusted with authority for such work.

Application was also made for permission to take rubbings of the sculpture on the Crosses. As the operation, though unattended with risks which have to be guarded against in the case of castings, would have involved resting ladders against the Crosses, the Board were reluctantly obliged to decline to give the requisite authorization. It is difficult to foretell the result of pressure against old and weather-worn monuments of this class, and in addition the shaft of one of the Crosses is known to extend very little below the surface of the ground.

The tumulus at New Grange, which is one of an important group of similar monuments in Meath, was vested in the Board in 1889, and in 1890 it was found necessary to undertake some works of conservation in connection with it. At that time some of the large bearing stones showed symptoms of breaking, and the front lintel of one of the side chambers was badly cracked. These signs of decay were carefully noted and watched. In 1895 the fractured portion of the lintel was supported by two oak blocks which kept it together until recently when more extensive cracks have been observed in it and other stones. It has been found necessary in consequence of this disintegration to support the stones in such a way that while they are retained in their original position there will be no danger of setting up any new strains.

The stones which are fractured are from the Silurian rocks, a geological formation to be found in the neighbourhood. The lines of fracture follow the stratification and also follow the line of the transverse or "slatey" cleavage which is a peculiarity of the geological formation to which the stones belong. The stones in the structure from the more distant basaltic area show no trace of fracture.

Injuries to Monuments.

We regret to have to report that a portion of the tracery work of one of the upright stones at the tumulus of New Grange was defaced by the cutting of an inscription across it. The provisions of the Act of 1882, enable the Board to institute a prosecution for the defacement of any ancient monument, but difficulties necessarily exist in identifying the offenders. Caretakers are employed at all the more important monuments vested in the Board, but owing to the fact that visitors occasionally come in large numbers, it is not always possible to exercise adequate supervision over the acts of each individual. The Board have to rely largely for the protection of the monuments on the public, and they are glad to bear testimony to the care taken by the great body of visitors to avoid causing injury. When harm is done it is in virtually every case the result of thoughtlessness, not malice, and it is felt that when attention is called to the cases of injury, happily rare, public opinion, and the reverence felt throughout Ireland for ancient and historical structures will prevent the recurrence of such incidents as we have had to refer to. A conviction was obtained in the case referred to.

The principal works of repair carried out during the year are referred to at p. 32.

Sea Fisheries (Ireland) Act, 1883, 46 and 47 Vic., c. 26.

This Act provided from the Irish Church Fund a sum of £250,000 to be expended on Fishery Piers and Harbours, by grant or loan. The greater part of the expenditure under the Act was made by grant.

The Board have been in correspondence with the Irish Government and in communication with the Inspectors of Fisheries as to the expenditure of the available balance.

The Act of 1883 was a graft on the previous statutes, beginning virtually with 9 Vic. c. 3, which regulated the expenditure of moneys granted or lent for Fishery Piers and Harbours. Up to the passing of the Fisheries (Ireland) Act, 1869, 32 and 33 Vic. c. 92, the Board of Works had certain duties with respect to Fishery interests which by the 8th Section of that Act were transferred to the Inspectors of Irish Fisheries. The 18th Section provided that the Inspectors should when directed by the Lord Lieutenant report for the information of this Board in regard to the necessity for and advantage to be derived by the Fisheries from any proposed work.

The Act of 1883 introduced a new element into the procedure. By the 8th Section it provided for the constitution of a Body to be styled "The Fishery Piers and Harbours Commission," consisting of the Inspectors of Fisheries, and of one other person who should be Chairman, to be appointed by the Lord Lieutenant. The Section made it the duty of the Commission to give such assistance to this Board as the Inspectors of Irish Fisheries had previously given in the execution of the Fishery Piers and Harbours Acts, and to confer with the Board with regard to the works proposed from time to time to be executed out of the Sea Fisheries Fund; and generally to aid in carrying the Act into effect, as the Lord Lieutenant should direct. It provided that the Board before reporting to the Treasury as to any proposed work should furnish to the Commission a copy of the plans and specifications; and that the Commission might make such observations relative to such plans, &c., for the information of the Treasury as they should think fit.

The special features of procedure under the Act of 1883 were as follows:—

(*a*.) A local inquiry by the Commission into the necessities of the district and the best means of meeting them by the construction of marine works. At these inquiries the Commission selected the site of the works to be executed.

(*b*.) The submission by the Board of Works to the Commission of specific inquiries on the following points:

1. The class of vessels to be accommodated.

2. Whether it was proposed that such vessels should be able to enter or leave at all weathers at dead low water of spring tide, and if not at what time or tide.

3. Whether vessels should be able to float at all times of tide. Number to be accommodated.

4. Width and length of wharf.

5. How much land, if any, required for drying nets, &c.

6. Width of approach road.

7. As to accommodation for row boats, if necessary.

8. Maximum sum recommended to be expended.

(*c*.) Answers to these queries from the Commission.

(*d*.) Preparation and submission to the Commission of plans by the Board of Works.

In 1889 a considerable time after the operations of the Commission under the Act had virtually ceased, that Body was dissolved by section 4 of the Public Works Loans Act of that year, 52 and 53 Vic. c. 71. The Board will, however, have the guidance of the Irish Government in the selection of localities to be benefited and in determining the kind of work to be executed with the moneys still available.

Shannon Navigation.

The quay wall of the Canal at Limerick, forming the terminal portion of the Shannon Navigation which was very old, had been for some time under special observation in consequence of signs of weakness. During the year it became necessary to remove and to rebuild it from the foundations for a length of about 40 feet. In the course of the work it was found that the foundations had been originally laid on branches, underneath which were five or six feet of mud, and below this a layer of turf. The remainder of the wall, about 300 feet, was taken down for about 6 feet from the top, and reconstructed with increased strength. A considerable part of the work was carried out in the year under report and the remainder since its termination.

The following works have been executed on the Shannon, with the object of facilitating the traffic created by the Shannon Development Company's service.

Killaloe.—To facilitate the interchange of passengers, &c., between the Shannon Development Company's steamers and the trains of the Waterford, Limerick and Western Railway Company a new landing stage was erected at a point adjoining the Railway jetty.

Williamstown.—An old landing stage situate at this point, which, owing to dilapidation and decay, had become unfit for use, was, under an arrangement made with the owner, removed, and a new and larger structure erected. In addition, guide piles were driven, some dredging done, and a number of rocks removed from the channel by which the landing stage is approached. Since the completion of these works, Williamstown has been made a place of call for the steamers, and the accommodation provided has been largely utilised by the residents in the district.

Rossmore.—As a point most convenient for the inhabitants of the neighbouring town of Woodford there has been constructed a timber pier with stone filling. A road connecting the pier with the county road is being constructed at the expense of the county. The pier was largely used during last season, and has proved a great convenience to the people of Woodford and the surrounding district. On the completion of the pier a temporary road was made available for the use of persons passing to and from the steamers by an arrangement made by the Agent to the Marquis of Clanricarde, on whose property the pier is situated.

Dromineer.—The pier which had been used at Dromineer by the Shannon Development steamers was an old wooden structure belonging to the Grand Canal Company. This, under an arrangement made by the Board with the Canal Company, was removed, and a new wooden pier erected. A concrete pathway which was much required to ensure the safety of passengers going to and from the steamers was also provided.

Rooskey.—A road has been constructed along the east bank of the Shannon connecting the wharf at Rooskey with the public road. This has been done for the purpose of the coach service between Rooskey and Drumod referred to on p. 10.

IV.—LOANS.

(1.) Loans secured on Undertakings, *e.g.* :—

For Inland Navigation, Harbours, Railways, &c., under 1 & 2 Wm. IV., c. 33.

For Labourers' Dwellings in Towns, and Housing of the Working Classes, under Acts of 1866, 1885, 1890, and 1893.

(2.) Loans secured on Rates, *e.g.* :—

To Grand Juries for Roads, Bridges, Piers, Harbours, Lunatic Asylum Buildings, Courthouses, Reformatories, and Industrial Schools.
For purposes sanctioned by the Public Health Act.
For Labourers' Dwellings under the Act of 1883.
For Dispensary Houses.
For Workhouse Buildings, &c.

(3.) Loans secured on Lands, *e.g.* :—

For Arterial Drainage Works.
For Arterial Drainage Maintenance.
To Owners for improvement of Lands, viz. :—Drainage, erection of Farm Houses and Buildings, of Dwellings for Agricultural Labourers; Planting for Shelter (10 Vic., c. 32, &c.)
To Tenants for improvement of their Holdings, viz. :—Drainage, and most of the purposes included in the previous service (44 & 45 Vic., c. 49).
For Purchase under Land Act, 1870.

(4.) Miscellaneous Loans, *e.g.* :—

Glebe Loans.
For National School Teachers' Residences.
For National Schools and Training Colleges.
For Seed Supply under Acts of 1880, 1890, 1895, and 1898.

(5.) Irish Church Fund Loans—secured on Rates or Lands.

The extent and variety of the purposes for which loans are made by the Board are made clear by the abstract of Accounts of Loans for Public Works given in Appendix (C), and by the remarks on the several services which precede the abstract. The following statement shows the different purposes for which loans have been sanctioned during the year 1898-9.

Total Number of Loans for each Class.	Purposes of Loans sanctioned 1898–99.	No.	Amount.	Total Amount for each Class.
6	Class I.—Loans secured on Undertakings.		£	£
	Labourers' Dwellings,	6	62,625	
				62,625
164	Class II.—Loans secured on Rates.			
	Loans to Counties :—			
	County Roads, Bridges, and Piers,	14	6,468	
	Lunatic Asylum Buildings,	31	116,780	
	Loans to Unions :—			
	Public Health Acts,	70	104,900	
	Labourers Acts,	39	46,458	
	Dispensary Houses,	9	7,460	
	Workhouse Buildings,	1	3,200	
				283,770
881	Class III.—Loans secured on Lands.			
	Land Improvement—Loans to Land Owners,	251	34,400	
	" " Occupiers,	630	45,764	
				80,846

ADVANCES, REPAYMENTS, AND ARREARS.

The earliest mention of Public Works Loans to be found in the Abstract submitted by the Board is in connection with the Statute 57 Geo. III., c. 34, passed in 1817. The total of all loan advances from that date to 31st March, 1899 (with certain loans made under special Acts before 1817), is £42,615,634.

The classified abstract in Appendix (F), pages 54 to 57, shows the portions of this amount which have been (1) repaid, (2) remitted, (3) written off from Local Loans Fund, or (4) which remain outstanding. The figures showing repayment, remission, &c., for the aggregate are as follows:—

	£
Total Repayments, ...	23,640,905
Total Remissions, ...	6,047,835
Written off from Local Loans Fund, . .	307,184
Outstanding Balances, . . .	8,739,667
	£42,[illegible]

The aggregate of outstanding balances is represented in the books of the Office by 29,597 open accounts. The loans generally are in course of repayment by half-yearly instalments.

The amount issued to borrowers in the year 1898-99 out of moneys advanced by the National Debt Commissioners for loan purposes was £661,798, as against £310,757 in 1897-98, and £557,338 in 1896-97.

Of the total amount issued of £661,798, £480,742 was advanced on the following Services:—

	£
Lunatic Asylums Buildings, .	244,525
Public Health, . . .	76,817
Labourers Acts, . . .	110,013
Seed Supply, &c., Act, 1898, .	49,387
	£480,742

The amounts received in the year were £371,533, in repayment of principal, and £274,211 in respect of interest, making together £843,744. Of the total, £806,194 was paid over by the Board to the National Debt Commissioners, and £39,550 to the Irish Land Commission in discharge of principal and interest of loans made out of the Irish Church Fund.

With regard to the whole Loans Service, the following table shows the payments in discharge of Loans, and the arrears of principal and interest for the last four years:—

—	Payments.	Arrears. Principal.	Arrears. Interest.	Arrears. Total.	Total Principal Outstanding. (excluding Amounts written off.)
	£	£	£	£	£
1895-96, . .	764,732	689,801	206,369	896,170	8,452,489
1896-97, . .	757,683	593,024	304,804	897,828	8,492,430
1897-98, . .	788,413	335,964	188,146	524,150	8,613,048
1898-99, . .	843,744	331,960	193,425	525,385	8,759,667

The following Abstract shows the amounts to which the arrears set forth in the above table have accrued on the various loan services:—

—	31st March, 1898. Principal.	31st March, 1898. Interest.	31st March, 1898. Total.	31st March, 1899. Principal.	31st March, 1899. Interest.	31st March, 1899. Total.	Principal Amount outstanding on 31st March, 1899.
	£	£	£	£	£	£	£
Public Works Loans generally, .	17,276	9,880	27,156	18,733	12,400	31,333	6,011,679
Public Health Acts, . . .	736	829	1,565	693	155	840	1,166,380
Railways, ...	269,787	160,132	410,919	255,127	153,760	408,888	433,809
Land Charges, payable by Owners,	34,646	21,173	56,819	33,689	31,111	64,800	(a) 2,036,879
Do. do. Occupiers,	10,563	5,545	16,108	11,553	5,622	17,175	626,231
Seed Supply Acts, . . .	12,964	–	12,969	12,343	–	12,343	83,889
	335,964	188,165	524,130	331,960	193,125	525,385	(b) 8,759,667

(a) Includes [illegible] Drainage Charges, payable by Occupiers. (b) Excluding Amount £307,4[illegible] written off from the Local Loans Fund.

Arrears on "Public Works Loans generally" show an increase of £4,016, accounted for by additional arrears on Harbour loans amounting to £4,625, there being a decrease in overdue instalments on other loans comprised under this head.

Of the entire increase, about £3,350 is due to causes of a temporary nature, such as delay connected with payment of Grand Jury presentments, and a considerable part of the remainder has arisen on a loan which is being remitted under agreement between the Treasury and the Harbour Commissioners of Wicklow.

Public Health Act arrears have been reduced from £1,362 to £980, and Railways from £410,219 to £403,369.

Arrears on Land Charges payable by owners, which had increased in 1897-98 to £65,819, as compared with £53,221 in the preceding year, show a decrease, the amount overdue being £[illegible].

The loans, made in the year under the Land Law Act, 44 and 45 Vic., cap. 49, sec. 31, brought the total advances to occupiers of land for the improvement of their holdings to £1,062,122. Of this sum £288,614 8s. 2d., principal, had been repaid, and £4,577 10s. 2d. written off the assets of the Local Loans fund as irrecoverable. There were arrears (principal) of £11,348 4s. 6d., and the balance, £685,562 12s. 11d., represented principal outstanding. The arrears have chiefly accumulated on the earlier loans. Out of the 740 Land Law Loans which are at present two gales or upwards in arrear, 16 represent the number of defaulters on loans made during the last five years. The total—principal and interest—in arrear on the service stood at £13,419 at the close of the year, as against £15,917 on March 31st, 1898. The increase this year over 1897-8 amounted to £502, being the smallest in any year since 1891. It may be regarded as consisting mainly of the additions caused by effux of time to accumulations on loans already in arrear for considerable periods.

Under the Seed Supply and Potato Spraying Machine Act of 1898, a sum of £36,388 was advanced during the year, bringing the total advances under this Act to £78,330, the number of Unions to which advances were made being 89.

The arrears on Seed Supply Loans at the close of the year were as follows:—Act of 1880, £9,626; Act of 1890, £812; Act of 1895, £1,703. Of the sum in arrear under the Act of 1880, £432 has been paid since 31st March, 1899. The principal represented by the balance, arose on loans made to Belmullet, Cahersiveen, Clifden, Dunfanaghy Glenties, Oughterard, Swinford, and Westport Unions.

Applications are occasionally made, sometimes under the Arterial Drainage Acts and sometimes under the Land Improvement Code, which, owing to the inapplicability of existing facilities, are generally either abandoned or refused. These are cases where works involving comparatively small cost are proposed in the interest of several proprietors or occupiers, in order to effect drainage, and where the parties interested desire to take common action and carry out such works for the common advantage on their respective lands, and sometimes in addition on the lands of persons who will derive little or perhaps no benefit from the proposed expenditure. Several applications of this class were made during the year, which so far as could be judged on the *primâ facie* case made would have resulted in considerable improvement if it had been practicable to proceed with them. Strictly speaking, such schemes come under the Arterial Drainage system, which creates machinery for united action, distributes the cost in proportion to the benefit conferred, and provides for the maintenance of the works to be executed.

The Board find difficulty in some instances in obtaining from applicants for Glebe Loans properly prepared plans and specifications. To obtain good work such plans and specifications are necessary, and the moderate outlay on architect's fees would be amply repaid. The Board are not at liberty to prepare plans in these cases. Their duty is confined to examining them when submitted, and seeing that no issue is made at foot of the loan until a corresponding amount of work has been carried out.

Kinsale Harbour, Co. Cork.—In the case of this harbour the Board made advances between the years 1885 and 1889, amounting to £11,352 13s. 1d., repayable in twenty-five years, with interest at 5 per cent. per annum. The loan is charged on the revenue of the harbour and on the rates of the town.

By Award, dated 23rd April, 1890, the debt became repayable in twenty-five years from the 1st November, 1889. The rate of interest was subsequently reduced to 4 per cent., it being provided that interest should be calculated at this rate from the time at which it began to accrue. The harbour revenue being insufficient to meet the charge, contributions from the town rates were paid under a mandamus in 1893 and subsequent years. In October, 1897, the Treasury authorised the Board to offer to the local authorities (1) a prolongation of the original currency of the loan (twenty-five years) by ten years, thus making the period of repayment twenty-seven years from 1st November, 1897, (2) a reduction of the outstanding principal by a sum of £1,000, both concessions being subject to the condition that the original terms as to period for repayment and amount due should revive in case of future default in meeting instalments of principal or interest. The conditions were accepted, and the concession is now in operation.

Sale of the Waterford, Dungarvan, and Lismore Railway.—This line (43 miles) was opened in 1878, having been built partly by a loan from the Board of £93,270, secured by mortgage and bearing interest at 4 per cent., and repayable by instalments in twenty years, partly by share capital, £230,000, raised on a guarantee (terminating in 1913) of interest at 5 per cent. given by the County and the City of Waterford, and partly with other moneys advanced on loan. After construction and original equipment, it was found necessary to provide additional rolling-stock to the value of about £28,000 on the hire system, the liability being arranged to be met by instalments of which the last was to fall due in 1904. A few years since the Company undertook the working of the Lismore and Fermoy line which connects the Waterford, Dungarvan, and Lismore with the Great Southern and Western Railway. Owing to the smallness of traffic, and to the necessity for expenditure out of revenue on renewals of the line, &c., not only was the Company unable to meet the capital instalments of the Board's loan, but arrears of interest amounting to £54,580 were due at the date of the sale.

Negotiations for sale of the Waterford, Dungarvan, and Lismore, and of the Fermoy lines to the Great Western Railway Company of England and the Great Southern and Western Railway Company were opened in 1897–98, and ended in the purchase of both railways by the Fishguard and Rosslare Railways and Harbours Company. This body was originally incorporated under the name of the Fishguard Railway and Pier Company in 1893; it acquired its present name in 1894 on the transfer to it of the undertakings of the Waterford and Wexford Railway Company and the Rosslare Harbour Commissioners. These undertakings were originally based on a project for connecting the South of Ireland with the Great Western Railway system of England by a service of steamers between Rosslare and Fishguard, and by the construction of a harbour at Rosslare, a railway connecting Rosslare with the Dublin, Wicklow, and Wexford line, and a railway connecting Wexford and Waterford city. The harbour at Rosslare and the line connecting that place with the Dublin, Wicklow, and Wexford Railway were completed, and in 1894 became vested in the Fishguard and Rosslare Railways and Harbours Company. The project for connecting Wexford and Waterford remained unaccomplished. In 1898, as the result of arrangements made between the Great Western and the Great Southern and Western Companies and the Fishguard and Rosslare Railways and Harbours Company, the last passed under the control of the two first-named bodies, and its directorate is henceforth to consist of four Directors of the Great Western Company and three of the Great Southern and Western Company.

The sale of the Waterford, Dungarvan and Lismore line was effected by an agreement between the Treasury and the Fishguard and Rosslare Harbours Company, executed on 31st July, 1898, and scheduled to the Fishguard and Rosslare Railways and Harbours Act, 1898 (61 & 62 Vict., cap. cclii.)

The effect of the agreement and the Act was that the Fishguard and Rosslare Company undertook the following obligations :—

1. Payment to the Treasury out of the first moneys raised under the powers of the Act, of £93,000, with interest thereon, at the rate of 2½ per cent. from the date of vesting of the line to the date of payment.

2. The construction, with the sanction of Parliament, of a line from Fermoy to a station (Dunkettle) on the Great Southern and Western Railway.

3. The construction, with the sanction of Parliament and the co-operation of the local authorities in Cork and certain Railway Companies west of Cork, of a line to connect these lines with the systems of the Great Southern and Western and the Fishguard and Rosslare Companies.

4. The construction of a line connecting Rosslare with the city of Waterford.

5. The construction of the last-mentioned railway at Waterford in such manner as to be consistent with the construction of certain authorised railways and works of the Dublin, Wicklow and Wexford Railway Company.

6. The relief of the ratepayers from one-half of the guarantee provided by the Waterford, Dungarvan and Lismore Act, 1873. This guarantee amounted to £14,000 per annum.

7. The provision of reciprocal traffic facilities between the railways of the Fishguard and Rosslare Company and the railways of all Companies forming junctions with them.

8. The fullest system of through booking between the railways of the Great Western Railway Company and the systems of the Fishguard Company and the Great Southern and Western Railway Company by the short sea route *via* Fishguard and Rosslare, with an effective service of trains on both the English and Irish sides, and a fast service of steamers across the Channel.

9. The provision by the Great Western Railway Company, unless and until Parliament should otherwise determine, of an effective steamboat service between Waterford and Milford or Fishguard.

10. The maintenance and development of the traffic upon the lines of the Fishguard and Rosslare Company to the satisfaction of the Treasury.

11. In view of the then contemplated amalgamations of the Waterford and Central Ireland, and the Waterford and Limerick Railway Companies respectively, with the Great Southern and Western Railway Company, the maintenance of the *status quo* of both such first-mentioned Companies pending the decision of Parliament upon such respective amalgamations.

The Treasury agreed, upon payment of £93,000, to accept that sum in discharge of all principal moneys and interest under the mortgage to the Board of Works, and upon being satisfied that half of the works upon each of the sections of the scheme between Rosslare and Waterford and between Fermoy and Dunkettle respectively had been completed to pay the Fishguard, &c., Company the sum of £50,000, and upon the certificate of the inspecting officer of the Board of Trade that the whole of the works have been completed to pay the Company the further sum of £43,000, making in all £93,000.

Finally the Treasury undertook to make such applications to Parliament as might be necessary to enable them to fulfil the obligations just stated.

In the present Session of Parliament the Fishguard, &c., Company have introduced a Bill seeking power to construct a line between Cork and Fermoy. This line is not identical with, but intended to be in substitution for the railway connecting the two places which was contemplated by the Act and Agreement of last Session. It differs from that line as regards the route chosen and the point of junction with the Great Southern and Western Railway system near Cork.

The Bill enables the Company, in constructing the bridge for carrying the Rosslare and Waterford line over the River Suir, to affix thereto a footway 6 feet wide to enable foot passengers to cross the bridge.

LEGISLATION IN 1898.

LOCAL GOVERNMENT (IRELAND) ACT, 1898, 61 & 62 VIC., c. 37.

This statute has an important bearing on our duties with reference to loans to Local Authorities. The provisions affecting such loans are contained partly in the Act, and partly in an Order in Council December 22nd, 1898, made under the Act entitled the "Application of Enactments" Order.

County Councils.—The borrowing power of a County Council is limited to one-tenth of the rateable value of the County. The limit can be exceeded where a Council obtains a Provisional Order of the Local Government Board, confirmed by Act of Parliament, authorising a larger indebtedness. The limitation does not apply to loans for the construction, &c., of Lunatic Asylums.

The previous consent of the Local Government Board is requisite to enable a Council to add to its loan indebtedness.

The Council is at liberty to borrow, either by issue of stock or on mortgage, if there be special reasons for the latter method. Where a Council has borrowed by issue of stock, it cannot borrow on mortgage unless the mortgage debt is to be repaid in a period not exceeding five years. When loans are made for purposes peculiar to a specific portion of a county, security may be taken on a part of the County Fund. The Local Government Board, with the consent of the Council, will fix the area of charge.

Reference must here be made to the Public Works Loans Act, 1898 (61 and 62 Vic., cap. 54, sec. 4) hereinafter more fully set forth, which gives the Board of Works power to lend for the purposes of any work for which the Council of a County, Borough, or District in Ireland is authorised to borrow.

Section 7 of the Local Government Act constitutes the Council a local authority for the purposes of the Technical Instruction Acts, 1889 and 1891 (52 & 53 Vic., c. 76, and 54 & 55 Vic., c. 4). The Council thus acquires a power to borrow for the purposes of those statutes.

Rural District Councils.—These bodies may be regarded in two aspects, (1) as taking the place of the Baronial Presentment Sessions (Act, sec. 27, 1), and (2) as Rural Sanitary Authorities (*Ibid.* sec., 27, 4).

In the former capacity they have no borrowing powers. Money borrowed from the Board of Works for District works will be advanced to the County Council.

As Rural Sanitary Authorities, Rural District Councils are clothed with the powers conferred on such authorities by the Public Health Acts (Local Government Act, s. 33), and loans for Public Health purposes will be made to them.

The security on which the Board will lend will be a mortgage creating a charge on the District Fund leviable from the area of charge and applicable to the payment of expenses incurred for sanitary purposes.

Loans under the Labourers' Acts, 1883 to 1896, will be made to the District Council as Rural Sanitary Authority. Such loans must be charged upon the entire District. (Act, s. 57, 4).

Poor Law Guardians.—The borrowing powers of Guardians, and the powers of the Board to lend to them, are dealt with by the 61st section of the Act. The ordinary limit to these borrowing powers is fixed at one-fourth of the annual rateable value of the Union; but the Local Government Board may extend the powers to double this limit. The section transfers certain powers to make advances to Guardians from the Public Works Loans Commissioners to the Board of Works.

The loans coming under the section are those under the Poor Relief (Ireland) Act, 1838, and any Acts amending the same, including the Medical Charities Acts. Loans for the purchase, &c., of Dispensaries and Dispensary Houses come within its scope through a provision in the Definition Section (109) of the Local Government Act, 1898.

Section 61, amongst other provisions, authorises loans for the creation of District Schools, and for structural improvement of Workhouses.

The security for loans made to Guardians will be the proportion of the Poor Rate payable to them by the County Council.

County Boroughs.—The Corporations of County Boroughs are given the borrowing powers of a County Council, and the Board have corresponding lending powers for works.

Urban District Councils.—The Urban District Council is constituted the Urban Sanitary Authority for the District, and its most important borrowing powers will be those exercisable under the Public Health code, which confers corresponding lending powers on the Board of Works. The security for loans to Urban District Councils will be the Municipal Rate.

In addition to the provisions bearing on loans, the Act contains others relevant to various functions of the Board.

Section 18 empowers the County Council, by agreement with the Board, to take over any marine work constructed or acquired under the Railways (Ireland) Act, 1896 (59 and 60 Vic., c. 34, and provides that a work so taken over shall be subject to the legislation as to maintenance, &c., affecting piers transferred to Counties under the Grand Juries Act, 1853 (16 and 17 Vic., c., 136). The section declares (sub-section 3) that the provisions respecting maintenance shall extend to reconstruction, according to the original or any new plan.

Section 19 (sub-section 1) provides that where any ancient monuments or remains, within the meaning of the section, are being dilapidated, &c., the County Surveyor shall report same to the Council, and the latter may prosecute under the Ancient Monuments Protection Act, 1882. Sub-section 2 enacts that the provisions of section 11 of the Act of 1882 (defining "ancient monuments"), and section 1 of the Ancient Monuments Protection (Ireland) Act, 1892, shall have effect as if they were re-enacted, with the substitution of "County Council" for "Commissioners of Works," but provides that this enactment shall be in addition to and not in derogation of the provisions of the said sections as respects the Commissioners of Works. The effect of sub-section 2 is to clothe the County Council as to any monument that may become vested in that body with powers and duties analogous to those of this Board. The relations borne by the Board to Ancient and National Monuments are stated at p. 18.

Section 20 enables the Local Government Board, with the consent of a Drainage Board, to make a Provisional Order for transferring to a County Council the business of such Board arising in the County.

Section 58 (Licence Duties and Local Grants), sub-section 4, contains the following provision affecting local authorities in respect of certain charges payable to the Board, and in respect of certain guarantees under legislation with the administration of which the Board is connected. It enacts that where the amount to be raised in any area by a County Council in the year to meet any railway or harbour charge connected with a guarantee given or transaction occurring before the Act, or two or more such charges, would exceed sixpence in the pound on the rateable value of the area, there may be paid to the Council out of the sum paid under the section to the Local Taxation (Ireland) Account, a sum equal to one-half of such excess to be applied in reduction of the said amount.

PUBLIC WORKS LOANS ACT, 1898.

(61 and 62 Vic., c. 54).

The 4th section enables the Commissioners of Public Works, if they think fit, to lend under the Public Works (Ireland) Acts, 1831 to 1886, for the purpose of any work for which the Council of a County, Borough, or District in Ireland, are authorised to borrow. It further provides that notwithstanding anything in the Acts mentioned the loan may be made for such times as the Commissioners think fit, not exceeding the term for which the borrowing Council are authorised to borrow.

SEED SUPPLY AND POTATO SPRAYING (IRELAND) ACT, 1898.

(61 and 62 Vic., c. 50).

This Act empowers the Board, on the recommendation of the Local Government Board, and with the sanction of the Treasury, to lend money to Boards of Guardians for the supply of Seed Potatoes, Seed Oats, and Potato Spraying Machines and Spraying material to occupiers of land unable through poverty to obtain such supplies.

Loans are made repayable by two equal instalments, the first to be paid on the 1st September, 1899, and the second on the 1st September, 1900. Interest at 2¾ per cent. is charged on the Irish Church Temporalities Fund, and the making of a loan creates a charge on the Poor Rate, without any mortgage.

KINGSTOWN TOWNSHIP (TRANSFER OF HARBOUR ROADS) ACT, 1898.

(61 & 62 Vic., c. 52.)

The object of this Act was to transfer to the Town Commissioners of Kingstown the property of the Commissioners of Kingstown Harbour in certain pieces of road and plots of ground, and to the Dublin, Wicklow, and Wexford Railway Company certain other pieces of road.

The pieces of road transferred to the Town Commissioners were (1) the Crofton and Harbour roads (upper level), with certain exceptions, and (2) portions of the Royal Marine and Crofton-terrace roads. The plots of ground transferred to the town were (1) two plots between the Victoria Baths and Eastern Pier, containing about 35 perches; (2) certain strips of land on the south side of the Dublin, Wicklow, and Wexford Railway, so far as the same were the property of the Harbour Commissioners. The transfer to the Railway Company consisted of portions of the Crofton and Harbour roads, the former for the extension of the Railway Station, and the latter for the widening of the Railway approach to Carlisle Pier.

The Commissioners composing the Board of Works are Commissioners of Kingstown Harbour, not *virtute officii*, but by the appointment of the Lord Lieutenant. The administration of the harbour is thus vested in them, and they are responsible for it, while the expenditure for works is made by them as Commissioners of Works.

The Town Commissioners took over under the Act the maintenance, repair, lighting, and watering of the roads transferred to them. Your Lordships have conveyed your readiness to seek annually from Parliament a contribution to these expenses of £100. The plots of ground near the Victoria Baths border on the sea, and their acquisition was regarded by the Town Commissioners as advantageous for the purposes of ornament and recreation. The strips on the south side of the Railway were taken over with the view of running a road parallel with the shore at a place where the public have at present to make a *détour* inland.

Beside the Acts above referred to, reports have been furnished to Your Lordships during the year 1898-99, on the following Bills so far as they affected the duties of the Board:—

Lisburn Town Commissioners Bill, 1899.

Belfast Water Bill, 1899.

Great Southern and Western and Waterford, Limerick, and Western Railway Companies' Amalgamation Bill, 1899.

Kingscourt, Keady, and Armagh Railway Bill, 1899.
Improvement of Land Bill, 1899.
Fishguard and Rosslare Railways and Harbours Bill, 1899.
Great Southern and Western Railway Bill, 1899.
Small Houses (Acquisition of Ownership) Bill, 1899.
Belfast Corporation Bill, 1899.
Dublin Corporation (Extension of City Boundaries) Bill, 1899.

We have the honour to be

Your obedient servants,

THOS. ROBERTSON.
H. O'SHAUGHNESSY.
GEORGE A. STEVENSON.

H. WILLIAMS, *Secretary*,
17th July, 1899.

APPENDICES.

APPENDIX (A).

DETAILS OF VOTED SERVICES.

PUBLIC BUILDINGS.

NAVAL AND MILITARY BUILDINGS.

Royal Hospital, Kilmainham.—The work requisite in connection with the renewal of that portion of the roof of the west front which has been dealt with, was completed by taking down and rebuilding two heavy chimney stacks and cross walls, on which the roof rested. These structures, which appear to have formed part of the original building, were discovered during the progress of the work on the roof to require complete renewal.

Royal Naval Reserve Battery, Kenmare.—A new small arms magazine has been built and a new drain to prevent flooding provided.

Royal Hibernian Military School.—The latrines being situated about sixteen feet below the play-shed and yard level, and only accessible by a long straight flight of granite stairs dangerous for boys, new latrines have been constructed on the ground level. The new arrangement is not only safer of access, but being at a higher level, it is better lighted, and it affords improved ventilation, while the foul air is carried away at a level that does not interfere with the adjoining play-sheds or grounds.

COAST GUARD STATIONS.

Killybegs, Co. Donegal.—A new semaphore has been erected, and the chimneys of the Divisional Officer's house rebuilt.

Bell Hill, Co. Donegal.—Twenty yards of retaining wall to approach have been built, and slope drained.

Inishsaffin, Co. Donegal.—Thirty feet of the lower end of boat-slip have been reconstructed.

Malin Head Co. Donegal.—A new store has been built.

Tribane, Co. Donegal.—Flagstaff foundations, new ceiling to boat-house, and new oak skids have been provided.

Blacksod, Co. Mayo.—The drainage has been improved, and new concrete banks provided.

Elly Bay, Co. Mayo.—Similar works executed.

Ross, Co. Mayo.—The difficulty in obtaining a site for the new boat-house has been overcome, and the erection is proceeding.

Roundstone, Co. Galway.—The boat-slip has been lengthened by forty feet.

Cushendun, Co. Antrim.—New station. This work, which was provided for in the estimates of the year, was not commenced owing to questions which arose as to the suitability of the site proposed to be acquired for the new station.

Strangford, Co. Down.—A new boat-house has been erected here for the use of the station.

Dunmore, Co. Waterford.—The erection of a Chief Officer's house was commenced under special Treasury sanction shortly before the end of the year.

Cashen River, Co. Kerry.—A new sanitary system has been introduced.

Castletownsend, Co. Cork.—A new sanitary system has been introduced.

Dunny Cove, Co. Cork.—A tender for building the new station for a chief boatman and seven men with an office was accepted by the Board in August, and the Contractor is progressing steadily with the works; two months almost continuous rain kept the works back considerably.

Arthurstown, Co. Wexford.—A contract was accepted for building a new station for a chief boatman and four men with an office, in August, and the work was practically completed before the end of the year.

State and Official Residences.

Viceregal Lodge.—The orchid and gardenia houses has been renewed.
The Lodge has been provided with a complete installation of electric bells.

Legal Departments.

Irish Land Commission.—Alterations to the strong-room shelving have been carried out. A complete installation of telephones has been introduced

Four Courts.—Extended sanitary accommodation has been provided for the public transacting business at the Courts.

Land Judges Department.—Provision of £100 was made for converting the Court into an office for the Chief Receiver, but it was decided, after reconsideration of the matter by the Judges not to proceed with the work. The Court remains available for judicial purposes, arbitrations, &c.

Science and Art Buildings.

Kildare-street Buildings.—The lighting of the herbarium and of the antique furniture room, which was insufficient, has been improved.
Requisite sanitary works have been carried out in the basement of Leinster House.
A dry area has been formed at the back of the Lancashire boilers in the basement of the Art Museum, and a new drainage system introduced.

Botanic Gardens, Glasnevin.—An extensive addition has been made to the fern house.

Dublin Metropolitan Police.

Manor-street Barrack and Station.—New wash house fittings have been introduced.

Donnybrook Barrack and Station.—A new store has been erected and the old store converted into a canteen.

Terenure Barrack and Station.—A new porch has been erected.

Booterstown Barrack and Station.—The roof of the Inspector's office and part of the main roof have been renewed.

Kingstown Barrack and Station.—Various sanitary improvements have been introduced and the sergeants' mess re-roofed.

Royal Irish Constabulary.

Farm Hill, Co. Mayo.—Sanitary improvements have been carried out.

Foxford, Co. Mayo.—The boundary walls have been newly coped and additional light and air to men's quarters secured by lowering inner wall of yard.

Fenagh, Co. Leitrim.—The drains have been relaid, and a portion of the wall lined with concrete.

Clonmany, Co. Donegal.—Some sanitary improvements have been introduced.

Londonderry.—Some concrete paving has been carried out.

Baldoyle, Co. Dublin.—The drainage has been improved and outfall extended.

National Education Buildings.

District and Minor Model Schools.

Londonderry.—A new paled fence to the plantation adjoining playground has been provided.

Albert Model Farm, Glasnevin.—The cow-house accommodation has been greatly improved, and new and improved fittings introduced.

A new Lecture Gallery and Demonstration bench and table have been erected primarily for the use of the Professor of Chemistry. They are also intended to be available for other lectures.

Lurgan and Monaghan District Model Schools.—The entire sanitary arrangements have been remodelled, the accommodation heretofore existing being of the kind in use when the buildings were originally erected.

Ordinary Literary Schools.

Aughadacor, Co. Donegal.—A new roof and ceiling have been provided.

Meenaladdy, Co. Donegal.—A new roof and ceiling have been provided.

Queen's Colleges.

Galway.—The Pharmacy and Materia Medica departments have been heated by hot water, the heating of other departments has been improved, and certain defects in hot water mains have been remedied.

Some sanitary works have also been carried out.

Belfast.—The entrance hall has been heated by the introduction of hot water, circulating in three large radiators.

In the *Natural History Museum* the exhibits having increased largely, the space originally provided was found much too small, and additional room has been provided by constructing a gallery around three sides of the apartment, with suitable wall cases, and a staircase leading thereto.

Post Office Buildings.

Postal and Telegraph Buildings, Dublin.—The protection of the buildings from fire has been improved at the General Post Office in Sackville-street, by introducing high pressure water mains, with fixed and instantaneous couplings and hose.

Coleraine, Navan, and Portadown.—Telegraph linesmen's huts have been provided.

Londonderry.—New fire appliances have been supplied.

A new pitch pine floor has been laid in the Sorting Office, and a screen and door provided across the passage to the instrument room.

Westport, Co. Mayo.—Tenders for the new office have been received.

Parsonstown, King's Co.—A new linesman's hut has been erected.

Castlerea, Co. Mayo.—A new linesman's hut has been erected.

Kingstown.—Extensive alterations and additions have been carried out. A new basket shed has been erected.

Rathmines.—A new basket shed has been erected.

Ballsbridge.—A new basket shed has been erected.

Belfast G.P.O.—The plans and specifications for contemplated alterations of the present office, rendered necessary by the removal of the Parcels' Post and certain other postal work to the new Parcels' Depot, were prepared, and tenders called for.

Newry Post Office.—This work had advanced so far in December last as to permit the entire of the rere portion of the building to be occupied. The Postal officials were thus enabled to use the sorting-room forming part of the rere to meet the pressure of the Parcels' Post business at Christmas. Delay has been caused in the completion of the front by the action which became necessary in order to arrange for the provision and supply of a local granite instead of the brick originally contemplated for the exterior. The foundation stone of the buildings was laid in January last.

Armagh and Dundalk.—Preliminary plans were prepared and submitted for approval to the Post Office Authorities early in the year, but the matter was not sufficiently advanced to allow of the preparation of contract plans, and consequently no money has been spent on these buildings during the year.

Lisburn.—Additions and alterations have been made to the fittings, and a new store room erected.

Kilkenny.—The public and sorting offices being too small for the increased business, it was decided to move the instrument-room from the ground to the first floor. In connection with this it was further found necessary to re-allocate the space generally on each floor, and to add a retiring room for clerks and messengers. The works have been fully completed.

Curragh Camp.—Shortly before the end of the year a site was secured at the Curragh Camp for a new Post Office, and plans of the new offices and residence for the Postmaster have been prepared.

Waterford.—The temporary Parcels Office erected here, almost exclusively of timber, at the initiation of the Parcel Post system, having become decayed, and being past repair, the ground and first floor of the stores adjoining, but no longer required by the Customs Department, were altered and adapted for Parcel Post service by inserting additional windows and doors, and by lowering the level of the ground floor. The old fittings modified and improved have been utilized for the new office. The removal of the temporary shed leaves ample yard space for driving to and from the Parcels Store, thereby saving time and affording greater facilities to the postal service.

Cork.—The site adjoining the public office in Pembroke-street, on which five shops stand, was acquired for the purpose of extending this post office. It is proposed to build a new letter sorting-room and parcels sorting-room on the newly-acquired site, with instrument-room, battery-room, and offices on the first floor, and kitchen and dining-room for the use of the staff on the top floor. Rooms for postmen, delivery clerks, and messengers, with a large yard, will occupy the position of the old parcels sorting-room, while the old letter sorting office will become a public office and clerks-room, etc.

The new building will correspond architecturally with the present building.

Royal Irish Academy.

The whole basement has been concreted.

Dundrum Criminal Lunatic Asylum.

About 300 feet of boundary wall has been taken down and rebuilt to a height of 16 feet.

Ordnance Survey Buildings.

Ennis.—Various improvements in the divisional sergeants' and messengers' quarters have been carried out.

Royal University.

All the roof lights except those on the small concert-room, have been renewed.

District Probate Court Registry Offices.

General Register Office, Dublin.—A new and separate room for the bookbinders has been erected.

Limerick Probate Office.—The strong-room, having hitherto been shelved with timber, was considered dangerous, and to render the room safe in case of fire the Board have had it fitted up with iron standards, shelving, and doors.

Londonderry Probate Office.—The lighting of the public office has been improved.

Local Registration of Title.

Additional strong-room accommodation has been provided in a convenient position in connection with the offices of this department.

DEPOSITORIES FOR PAROCHIAL RECORDS.

(Act 39 and 40 Vic. c. 58.)

Under the provisions of this Act inspections of proposed Depositories have been made in eight cases, and reports thereon forwarded to the Deputy Keeper of the Records.

Inland Revenue Buildings, Dublin.

Alteration in Stamping Room.—This work, which consisted in a re-arrangement of the whole interior of the office, has been satisfactorily completed. It affords greater security and protection for the stamping apparatus, with increased space and facility for the public transacting business in this department.

Public Gardens, &c.

Phœnix Park and Stephen's Green, Dublin, and the Curragh of Kildare.

The usual works of maintenance and repair in connection with the buildings, roads, grounds, &c., have been carried out. Improvements to the paths and sitting accommodation on the side of the main road opposite the People's Garden, Phœnix Park, were undertaken and are in progress. In Stephen's Green a kiosk, which will afford considerable sitting accommodation and shelter, was commenced in the year and completed since its termination.

Royal Harbours.

A summary of the rainfall and tidal observations at Kingstown, and remarks by the Harbour Masters on the Fishing Industry and Trade at the several harbours, will be found in Appendix (D).

Kingstown Harbour.—A breach in the sea-slope near the pier head (East Pier) was repaired by removing heavy rubble and replacing it encased in a mass of concrete, forming a solid base to the slope above it. Two minor breaches were repaired in the same manner.

Extensive filling, tucking, and pinning with concrete, was done on the lower reach of the West Wharf wall (West Pier).

At the Carlisle Pier new piling for the protection of the west side was carried out.

The outer side of the coal quay was found on examination by divers to be somewhat undercut. A footing course of concrete has been laid down at the outer side of it, above which the masonry is being underpinned.

Dredging—No. 1 Dredger.—The total quantity dredged (between the Victoria Wharf and the mouth of the harbour) was 54,480 tons. The dredger underwent extensive repairs during the winter.

No. 2 Dredger dredged at the foot of the lifeboat slip, along the front of the Victoria Wharf, and at the West Pier stone berths. Quantity dredged, 5,087 tons.

A carpenter's shop and a substantial shed were constructed in the harbour yard, the latter in connection with the band saw.

Her Majesty's ships, the vessels of the Irish Lights Board, and trading vessels were supplied with water, and ballast was supplied to the last-mentioned class. The City of Dublin Company's steamers are no longer supplied by the Board, but contract with the Local Authority.

Howth Harbour.—The breakwaters and other works were duly maintained, and 5,268 tons of silt were dredged by Dredger No. 2.

Ardglass and Donaghadee Harbours, Co. Down, and Dunmore East Harbour, Co. Waterford.—The breakwaters, roads, buildings, and other works were duly maintained.

Shannon Drainage.

The sluices have been maintained in good order.

River Maigue Navigation.

The Collector's house and bridge have been duly maintained.

Ancient Monuments.

See pages 16 and 17 and 26.

APPENDIX (B).

DETAILS OF NON-VOTED SERVICES.

Arterial Drainage and Improvement of Lands (Ireland) Act, 1863, and Amendments.

26 & 27 Vic., c. 88; 27 & 28 Vic., c. 72; 28 & 29 Vic., c. 52; 32 & 33 Vic. c. 79; 35 & 36 Vic., c. 31; 37 & 38 Vic., c. 32; 41 & 42 Vic. c. 59; 43 & 44 Vic., c. 27; and 55 & 56 Vic. c. 65.

The works of the Bunkey District, Co. Tipperary, were completed, and those of the Carrigrohane District, Co. Cork, were brought near completion before the end of the year. They have since been finished.

A schedule of the final awards made under the Acts will be found in Appendix (G), pages 82 to 97.

The total area of land drained or improved in the districts dealt with by these awards is 128,638 statute acres, and the total cost chargeable thereto amounts to £908,040. This has been in addition to the works of the Drainage districts carried out under the Act 5 and 6 Vic., c. 89, and the Acts amending it, between the years 1842 and 1860. By these earlier works a total of 266,736 acres was drained or improved. A statement as to the expenditure on Arterial Drainage will be found in Appendix (G), p. 82, *infra*.

Increased Rents in respect of Arterial Drainage Rent Charges.

Drainage Maintenance, 29 and 30 Vic., c. 49, &c.

Inspections were made in the cases of the Lough Erne District, Counties Fermanagh, Cavan, Donegal, and Monaghan; Inland Lakes and Glore River District, County Mayo; Inny District, Counties Longford and Westmeath; Upper Inny District, Counties Cavan, Longford, Meath, and Westmeath. Communications regarding the maintenance of these works were made to the Trustees of the several Districts.

Maintenance of Navigation Works.

19 and 20 Vic., c. 62.

No works have been carried out under this Act during the year.

Railway Clauses Consolidation Act.

8 Vic., c. 20, sec. 15.

Certificates of the dimensions of Culverts and Waterways were issued in the following cases:—

Londonderry and Lough Swilly Railway, Burton Port Extension.
Donegal Railway, Strabane to Londonderry Extension.
Sutton to Howth Electric Tramway.

Fishery Piers and Harbours Maintenance.

16 & 17 Vic., c. 136.

Repair works were carried out at Ard West Pier, County Galway, during the year, at a cost of £500. Inspections were made at Kilmore Pier, County Wexford, Castletown Berehaven, County Cork, and Kilkeel Pier, County Down, in connection with the maintenance of these works, and the County Authority communicated with.

Sea Fisheries (Ireland) Act, 1883.

See pp. 17 and 18.

Shannon Navigation.

In addition to the works on the Navigation reported at p. 19, a new wharf was erected at Limerick for the timber trade. Dredging was done at Banows, Killaloe, Portumna, Banagher, Shannon Bridge, Athlone, and Dromod. The old breakwater at Dromod was removed in order to improve the approach to the Quay. The Military Pier at Athlone was (with the consent of the Military Authorities), made available for use by the Shannon steamers. The jetty at Portumna was improved. At Banagher a new pathway was constructed between the Quay and the Railway Station. Four new buoys were put down at Kilgarvan to improve the marking of the deep water channel. A new Collector's house was built at Athlone. The locks, bridges, tow-paths, buoys, &c., were duly maintained.

County Road Maintenance.

6 & 7 William IV., c. 116, sec. 61.

No inquiry under the provisions of the above Act was held during the year.

Post Roads.

6 & 7 William IV., c. 116, sec. 61.

An application from the Postmaster-General was received for repairs to the road from Glenbeam to Graigue, County Cork. The repairs were undertaken by the County Authorities from funds advanced by this Board, to be repaid by levies on the county. Another application was received for the repair of the post road between Ballina and Belmullet by the rebuilding of Muania Bridge. In this case the Board recommended that, pending the passing of the Local Government Act, the bridge should be temporarily repaired.

Arklow Harbour.

The Board's dredger No. 2 was let to the Arklow Harbour Commissioners, and dredged 3,193 tons from the harbour.

Royal Canal.

A considerable amount of work of the class recommended by the Board of Trade has been carried out by the Midland Great Western Railway Company, including dredging on the 3rd, 17th, 39th, and 40th levels, and at Spencer Dock and sea-lock. Weeds have been cut and removed throughout the Canal. Several lock gates have been renewed, and others repaired. The condition of the Canal is generally improved since the Board of Trade inspection of 1894.

Road Presentments.

16 and 17 Vic., c. 136.

The presentment of the County Antrim Grand Jury for the construction of a new road from Larne to Ballymena was duly approved by this Board.

Cleggan, County Galway.

An application with reference to the proposed improvement of this Harbour was investigated.

National Monuments.

See pp. 15 and 26.

Land Improvement Act, 1864. Limited Owners' Residences Acts, 1870, &c.

27 & 28 Vic., c. 113; 33 & 34 Vic., c. 56; 34 & 35 Vic., c. 84; 40 & 41 Vic., c. 31.

Five applications have been made to the Board during the past year for sanction to expenditure under these Acts as against seven in 1897-8. The total sum covered by these applications was £4,705, being a decrease of £5,319 on the previous corresponding period. Most of the recent applications of this class have been presented to the Board through a Society which lends for the purposes of the Land Improvement Statutes. One Provisional Order authorising the commencement of work, and seven Absolute Orders in cases where works were completed have been issued, the latter dealing with charges on estates amounting to £7,157 16s. 1d., as against three Absolute Orders for £793 4s. 9d. during the preceding year.

ARBITRATIONS UNDER "THE RAILWAYS (IRELAND) ACTS" (1851, 1860, 1864).

14 & 15 Vic., c. 70; 23 & 24 Vic., c. 97; and 27 & 28 Vic., c. 71.

Arbitrations have been applied for and Arbitrators appointed in the following cases, viz.:—

Railway Companies:

Donegal Railway Company—Lands required in Londonderry.
Great Southern and Western Railway—Lands required in Mallow and Drumcondra.
Great Northern Railway—Lands required in County Dublin.

Corporations:

Belfast Water Commissioners Waterworks.
Rathmines and Rathgar Improvement Commissioners—Lands required for widening streets.
Trustees of St. Patrick's Park, Dublin—Lands required in Dublin.
Trustees of Drumard National School—Site for school.

INQUIRIES INTO TRAMWAY PROJECTS.

23 & 24 Vic., c. 152, s. 9; 24 & 25 Vic., c. 102, ss. 6, 7.

The Board held inquiries into the engineering merits of the following undertakings, viz.:—

Ballinphelic and Carrigaline Tramway and Light Railway.
Limerick Electric Tramways.
North Down Tramways (Bangor to Donaghadee).
Lucan and Leixlip Tramways.

APPENDIX (C).

DETAILS OF LOAN SERVICES, WITH ABSTRACT OF ACCOUNTS AND TABLES.

CLASS (1).—LOANS SECURED ON UNDERTAKINGS.

Labourers' Dwellings in Towns and Housing of the Working Classes.

Nos. 7 and 8 in Abstract, p. 54.

Labouring Classes Dwellings (Ireland) Act, 1866 (29 & 30 Vic., c. 44); and the Housing of the Working Classes Acts, 1885, 1890, and 1893 (48 & 49 Vic., c. 72, and 53 and 54 Vic., c. 70).

Amount of loans sanctioned under Act of 1866, while it continued operative, *i.e.*, to the close of the year 1884-85—£281,334. Number of dwellings erected—3,416. Rate of Interest charged—4 per cent.

During the year 26 applications have been received for loans under the Housing of the Working Classes Act, 1890, the total amount applied for being £38,158 18s. 1d. Eight loans amounting to £49,655 have been sanctioned, as against 4 loans to the amount of £15,836 sanctioned during the previous year.

The following table shows the number and amount of the loans made each year since 1866, when the first of these Acts was passed.

Year,	No. of applications sanctioned.	Amount sanctioned.		No. of families to be accommodated.
		£	s.	
1866-67, .	Nil	—		Nil.
1867-68, .	1	625	0	8
1868-69, .	Nil	—		Nil.
1869-70, .	1	800	0	10
1870-71, .	1	4,166	0	128
1871-72, .	3	1,660	0	46
1872-73, .	8	7,173	0	106
1873-74, .	7	22,230	0	261
1874-75, .	1	910	0	12
1875-76, .	7	24,263	0	259
1876-77, .	5	11,100	0	132
1877-78, .	6	22,811	0	672
1878-79, .	10	7,100	0	61
1879-80, .	19	31,836	0	251
1880-81, .	17	28,870	0	307
1881-82, .	17	23,674	0	458
1882-83, .	15	71,187	0	570
1883-84, .	16	40,033	0	597
1884-85, .	12	27,264	0	338
1885-86, .	20	30,760	0	719
1886-87, .	24	79,181	0	863
1887-88, .	20	24,716	10	297
1888-89, .	25	52,762	10	478
1889-90, .	15	46,819	0	603
1890-91, .	20	42,413	0	628
1891-92, .	11	10,164	0	138
1892-93, .	6	44,370	0	451
1893-94, .	7	11,483	0	86
1894-95, .	9	36,209	0	163
1895-96, .	7	16,170	0	211
1896-97, .	12	63,247	0	758
1897-98, .	6	13,838	0	137
1898-99, .	8	40,486	0	532
Total, .	326	856,110	0	—

Class (2).—Loans secured on Rates.

The number and the amount of the loans sanctioned under this head show a diminution which is accounted for by decreases on Asylum loans, and loans under the Labourers, and Public Health Acts.

—	1897-98.	1898-99.
Number of Loans, . .	375	351
Amount of Loans, . .	£420,567	£298,230

Loans for Works carried out by Grand Juries. Nos. 9 and 10 in Abstract, p. 54.

Loans for works carried out by Grand Juries show £6,403 sanctioned in 1898-99 as against £600 in 1897-98.

Public Libraries. No. 11 in Abstract, p. 54.

No loans have been advanced for the purposes of Public Libraries during the past year, although the Board have been in correspondence with several Local Authorities, which had it in contemplation to apply for advances. The maximum rate leviable for Library purposes under the Public Libraries Acts is one penny in the pound, and it is probable that in many localities the revenue derivable from such a rate would not cover working expenses, together with the annual charge which a loan would entail.

Industrial Schools and Reformatories. No. 11 in Abstract, p. 54.

No applications have been made for advances for Industrial Schools or Reformatories.

District Schools. No. 1 in Abstract, p. 54.

Under the Board's principal Act, 1 & 2 Wm. IV., c. 33, a loan of £1,700 has been applied for and made for a water supply to a District School established in pursuance of the Poor Law Act, 11 & 12 Vic., c. 25, for pauper children in the Unions of Croom, Kilmallock, Limerick, Listowel, Newcastle, and Rathkeale.

Loans for Asylum Buildings. No. 17 in Abstract, p. 54.

The number of loans sanctioned for Asylum buildings during the year was thirty-one, being an increase of seven over those of the previous period. The amount sanctioned was £114,504, as compared with £236,950 in the preceding year. The Local Government (Ireland) Act introduces a radical change in connexion with these loans, which have heretofore been expended under the supervision of the Board of Control of Lunatic Asylums. This Board, under Section 9 of the Statute, ceased to exist shortly after the end of the year, and loans will in future be expended by the local authority. As long as the supervision of expenditure of moneys raised on loan from the Board rested with the Board of Control, the Accountant's Department of the Board of Works kept the accounts of such expenditure, in addition to keeping the accounts dealing with the indebtedness of the borrowing County or District to the Board. The former class of accounts will henceforth be kept by the local authority responsible for the expenditure of the moneys lent.

Loans for Workhouse Buildings. No. 23 in Abstract, p. 54.

In 1866 the demands for increased workhouse accommodation having previously ceased, the Treasury directed that no further advances should be made from public moneys for workhouse buildings. For many years no loans were made for works at these buildings, except where the proposed work was necessary in the interest of the public health of the neighbourhood, as in the case of sanitary improvements, and in such instances the advances were made under the Public Health Act, 1878. We have stated (p. 26) the provisions of the Local Government (Ireland) Act, sec. 61, which give the Board power to lend for structural work at workhouses, among other purposes. Three applications for loans, amounting to £4,986 15s., were made during the year under review. Of these one received Treasury sanction before the close of the year, and is under issue.

Loans under the Public Health Acts. Nos. 19 and 39 in Abstract, pp. 54 and 56.

Loans under the Public Health Act of 1878 reached in number 70, and amounted to £104,919, as against the corresponding figures 60 and £114,776 for the previous year. The following table contrasts the two years in detail:—

PURPOSE.	1897-98.		1898-99.	
	Number of Loans.	Amount.	Number of Loans.	Amount.
		£		£
Water Works,	26	49,040	26	47,084
Sewerage,	13	7,376	14	7,638
Buildings, Public Lighting, Markets,	16	18,510	21	33,478
Streets, Paving, &c.,	5	39,850	9	16,468
	60	£114,776	70	£104,959

The total amount of loans authorised for sanitary purposes stood at £2,729,568 on 31st March, 1899, and the total amount issued at £2,639,007.

The distribution of the sum authorised between different sanitary purposes is as follows:—

	£
Water Works, ...	1,241,433
Sewerage, ...	410,023
Streets, Paving, &c., ...	601,777
Buildings, Public Lighting, Cemeteries, Parks, Markets,	476,616
	£2,729,548

Labourers Acts. No. 21 in Abstract, p. 54.

Loans were sanctioned under the Labourers Acts, 1883 and 1885, for sums amounting to £46,458 as against £60,616 in 1897-98. The sanctions from the commencement of the service as follows:—

	£
1884–88, ...	630,919
1888–89, ...	185,749
1889–90, ...	89,802
1890–91, ...	106,437
1891–92, ...	50,158
1892–93, ...	117,998
1893–94, ...	48,390
1894–95, ...	100,193
1895–96, ...	116,367
1896–97, ...	123,076
1897–98, ...	60,616
1898–99, ...	46,455

The loans sanctioned under these Acts amounted at the end of the year under report to £1,962,373. One hundred and nine out of 159 Unions had borrowed this sum; the remaining Unions had not up to that date availed themselves of the powers given by the Acts. The number of Unions which had borrowed, with the amount sanctioned in each Province, appears from the following figures:—

			£
Munster, . .	64	Unions, .	1,088,311
Leinster, . .	20	" .	633,038
Connaught, . .	8	" .	14,913
Ulster, . .	17	" .	47,087
	109		£1,962,373

The advances under the Acts in 1898–99 amounted to £110,018 bringing the total advanced to £1,782,985.

Loans for Dispensary Houses: No. 22 in Abstract, p. 54.

Twelve memorials, for an aggregate sum of £9,800, have been received during the year, as compared with seven, for £6,090, in the previous twelve months. We have pointed out (p. 25), the provisions of the Local Government (Ireland) Act, 1898 (Sec. 61), affecting this class of loans.

Class (3).—Loans secured on Lands.

This class comprises, in addition to loans made to tenants for purchase of their holdings, in accordance with the provisions of the Land Act of 1870 (under which no advances are now made), the following loans, having for their object the improvement of land:—

(a.) Loans for arterial drainage under 5 & 6 Vic., c. 89.

(b.) Loans made for arterial drainage works (26 & 27 Vic., c. 88), and loans made for the maintenance of such works (29 & 30 Vic., c. 49).

(c.) Loans to "owners" of lands for improvements, under 10 Vic., c. 32, and amending Acts, and under sec. 19 of 41 & 42 Vic., c. 49.

(d.) Loans to occupiers of lands for improvements, under sec. 31 of the Land Law Act, 1881, 44 & 45 Vic., c. 49.

Loans for Arterial Drainage. Nos. 24, 25, 26, and 44 in Abstract, pp. 54 and 56.

From 1842 to 1863 loans for Arterial Drainage were made under 5 and 6 Vic., c. 89. £2,092,059 was lent under this statute, the greater part during and after the famine of 1849. Of this amount £1,207,589 was remitted, and £874,447 repaid. The principal unpaid amounts to £23.

From 1863 loans for this purpose have been made under the Drainage and Improvement of Lands Act (Ireland), 1863, 26 and 27 Vic., c. 88, and amending Acts. The entire amount of such loans up to March 31, 1898, is £840,713, including £6,136 lent out of the Irish Church Fund.

Loans for Land Improvement, 10 Vic., c. 32; 13 & 14 Vic., c. 31; 29 & 30 Vic., c. 40, &c., No. 27 in Abstract p. 56.

The following table gives (1) the number of applications for loans and the amounts issued under the Land Improvement Acts in each year, from 1847, when this service commenced, to 31st March, 1899; (2) similar information as to "Land Law" loans, under sec. 31 of the Land Law Act of 1881 (made principally to tenants), from 1881 to 31st March, 1899.

The figures as to the last-mentioned loans should, strictly speaking, come under the head relating to them (p. 44), but it has been considered desirable to present in one view the operation of both services, which have a common object.

Land Improvement Acts, 10 Vic., c. 32, &c.

Year.	No. of Applications.	Amounts Issued.	Year.		No. of Applications.	Amounts Issued.
		£				£
1847, June to Dec. (inclusive).	1,384	72,790	1865,		90	46,318
1848,	871	286,160	1866,		84	38,783
1849,	618	378,836	1867,		143	79,180
1850,	490	250,334	1868-9,		179	64,878
1851,	250	145,453	1869-70,		166	65,778
1852,	161	88,143	1870-71,		179	77,880
1853,	144	53,434	1871-72,		180	63,635
1854,	183	49,793	1872-73,		223	78,290
1855,	96	33,160	1873-74,		234	99,873
1856,	106	52,810	1874-75,		246	102,001
1857,	114	61,674	1875-76,		265	98,720
1858,	118	35,134	1876-77,		318	191,408
1859,	111	39,334	1877-78,		278	131,348
1860,	138	36,905	1878-79,		310	150,870
1861,	184	36,658	1879-80,	Relief, . . 2,164 Ordinary, 463	2,627	a 334,810
1862,	184	42,373				
1863,	139	38,830	1880-81,		652	a 786,058
1864,	133	58,430				

LAND IMPROVEMENT ACTS, 10 VIC., c. 32, &c.—(continued) AND LAND LAW ACT, 1881.

Year.	Land Improvement Acts, 10 Vic., c. 32, &c.		Land Law Act, 1881, 44 and 45 Vic., c. 49	
	No. of Applications.	Amounts Issued.	No. of Applications.	Amounts Issued.
		£		£
1881–82, . . .	401	a 738,462	}	
1882–83, . . .	451	a 136,536	} 5,658	169,768
1883–84, . . .	503	a 122,067	}	
1884–85, . . .	385	a 117,160	2,758	211,403
1885–86, . . .	226	ab 79,678	1,935	110,643
1886–87, . . .	219	ab 66,191	911	74,449
1887–88, . . .	181	b 45,751	645	50,759
1888–89, . . .	148	b 31,793	418	33,641
1889–90, . . .	169	b 35,677	520	38,4[illegible]
1890–91, . . .	215	b 32,754	737	43,960
1891–92, . . .	227	b 30,804	526	41,565
1892–93, . . .	293	33,871	987	48,615
1893–94, . . .	276	33,331	748	41,157
1894–95, . . .	348	33,593	775	38,[illegible]
1895–96, . . .	303	b 34,377	796	37,043
1896–97, . . .	303	b 50,453	729	52,803
1897–98, . . .	347	44,019	787	52,077
1898–99, . . .	344	38,677	926	35,043

(a) Including Relief of Distress Loans. (b) Including Loans under 31st Section of the Land Law (Ireland) Act, 1881.

The business done under the Land Improvement Acts reached its lowest point in number of applications in 1888 89. Since that year there has been a decided though not continuous increase. The number of applications received during the year 1898-99 was 344 under the Land Improvement Acts; and 926 under the 31st sec. of the Land Law (Ireland) Act, 1881. Nearly one-half of the applicants under the Act 10 Vic., c. 32, were purchasers under the Land Purchase Acts. The tendency of this class to avail itself of loans under the Land Improvement Acts continues to increase.

The following particulars relate exclusively to loans under 10 Vic., c. 32:—

Classification of loans under which works were commenced in 1898-99:—

Class of Work.	No. of Loans under which Works were commenced.	Amount Sanctioned.	Average of each Loan.
		£	£
Drainage and other Land Works, . .	35	5,965	158
Farm Buildings, ...	210	31,080	152
Labourers' Cottages, ...	11	1,770	161
Mixed Loans—including Buildings and Land Works, ...	6	1,400	175
Totals, ...	262	40,215	—
General Average per Loan, .	—	—	153

The following table shows the certified expenditure on the various classes of works under loans completed during the year ending 31st March, 1899:—

	£	s.	d.
Field Works, . . .	3,972	9	4
Farm Buildings, . . .	36,643	11	0
Labourers' Cottages, . . .	1,537	0	0
Scutch Mills, . . .	—		
Planting for Shelter, . . .	—		

The following table gives the number of Land Improvement loans made, and the sums issued in the several counties of Ireland up to the 31st March, 1899:—

SCHEDULE showing the NUMBER of LOANS and AMOUNTS ISSUED from commencement of ACT.

Name of County.	No. of Loans.	Amount issued.	Total No. of Loans.	Total Amount issued.
		£ s. d.		£ s. d.
NORTHERN DIVISION.				
Antrim,	726	106,203 0 0		
Londonderry,	199	73,585 0 0		
Donegal,	631	100,641 0 0		
Fermanagh,	190	80,883 0 0		
Tyrone,	317	148,980 0 0		
Armagh,	6	26,316 0 0		
Down,	173	91,158 0 0	1,480	789,980 0 0
MIDLAND AND EASTERN.				
Cavan,	303	83,638 0 0		
Monaghan,	113	46,143 0 0		
Longford,	345	153,906 0 0		
Louth,	123	47,644 0 0		
Meath,	176	110,679 0 0		
Westmeath,	312	162,546 0 0		
Dublin,	316	97,783 0 0		
Kildare,	331	149,833 0 0		
King's,	290	89,318 0 0		
Queen's,	378	180,748 0 0		
Wicklow,	271	128,890 0 0		
Carlow,	332	109,440 0 0		
Kilkenny,	[illegible]	74,737 0 0		
Wexford,	463	133,613 0 0	3,977	1,854,795 0 0
WESTERN.				
Sligo,	383	150,535 0 0		
Leitrim,	203	76,105 0 0		
Mayo,	576	222,731 0 0		
Roscommon,	460	321,497 0 0		
Galway,	831	389,797 0 0		
Clare,	640	177,097 0 0	3,067	1,316,804 0 0
SOUTHERN.				
Limerick,	922	391,350 0 0		
Tipperary,	765	376,266 0 0		
Waterford,	276	88,819 0 0		
Cork,	1,513	441,737 0 0		
Kerry,	845	477,851 0 0	4,327	1,688,439 0 0
		Totals,	13,611	£5,980,330 0 0

Main and Thorough Drainage or other Field Works.

The number of Land Improvement loans sanctioned for works, of which thorough drainage or other field works forms the principal part, since the commencement in 1847 to the 31st March in this year, is 6,837, for £3,742,812, and of this number 28, for an aggregate of £5,310, were approved during the year ended 31st March, 1899.

Planting for Shelter.

Since the passing of the Act 29 and 30 Vic., c. 40, under which advances are made for this purpose, 132 loans, amounting to £30,550, have been made. Of this number, one loan for £800 was sanctioned during the current year.

Farm Buildings.

Under this head 3,965 loans have been sanctioned since the passing of the Act 10 and 11 Vic., c. 19, the amount being £1,327,400. This includes 215 loans, for an aggregate of £26,805, approved during the past financial year.

Dwellings for Agricultural Labourers.

For this class of work the number of loans sanctioned since the passing of the Act 28 Vic., c. 19, which first authorised such advances, is 615, for £383,470, of which 12 loans, amounting to £1,560, were approved in the year.

Under section 19 of the Land Law (Ireland) Act, 1881, we have power to make advances to tenant farmers, who, pursuant to the injunctions of the Irish Land Commission, and as a condition attached to the fixing of a "fair rent," proceed to erect labourers' dwellings on their holdings. Such tenants are deemed to be persons to whom a loan may be made under the Landed Property Improvement (Ireland) Acts, for the improvement or building of dwellings for labourers, as if they were owners within the meaning of the Act 10 Vic., c. 32, sec. 7. No loan was sanctioned under the 19th section of the Land Law Act, within the year ending 31st March, 1899. Two hundred and sixty such loans, amounting to £15,275, have been sanctioned under the Act since it came into operation, the instalments issued amounting to £13,880.

Advances for this purpose are also made under section 31 of the Land Law Act, 1881. See Table of Expenditure under this section, p. 45.

The following table shows the number and amount of Loans sanctioned for Dwellings for Agricultural Labourers under the Act 28 Vic., cap. 19, and the Land Law (Ireland) Act, 1881, sec. 19, since the passing of the Labourers' Acts, 1883 and 1885.

Year.	28 Vic., c. 19.		Land Law (Ireland) Act, 1881, sec. 19.	
	No. of Loans Sanctioned.	Amount Sanctioned.	No. of Loans Sanctioned.	Amount Issued.
		£		£
1883, . . .	37	13,210	28	333
1884, . . .	36	12,496	61	1,518
1885, . . .	35	6,915	84	5,039
1886, . . .	28	7,585	37	3,599
1887, . . .	18	6,100	11	1,485
1888, . . .	19	6,365	31	419
1889, . . .	13	5,070	3	113
1890, . . .	11	3,005	1	231
1891, . . .	17	4,665	6	271
1892, . . .	10	1,940	2	159
1893, . . .	20	5,005	Nil.	118
1894, . . .	14	4,385	Nil.	79
1895, . . .	21	4,770	1	4
1896, . . .	21	4,610	1	84
1897, . . .	13	2,015	1	105
1898, . . .	12	4,810	Nil.	5
1899, . . .	12	1,560	Nil.	Nil.

Loans to Tenants for Improvement of Holdings, or "Land Law Loans."

Land Law (Ireland) Act, 1881, Section 31. No. 29 in Abstract, p. 56.

The great body of loans to tenants are made under this provision. The number sanctioned under it during the year was 830, and the amount covered by these sanctions was £45,745, while the sums issued during the year reached £38,943. The total number of loans sanctioned under the section from the date of the Act to 31st March, 1899, is 14,292. The aggregate of amounts sanctioned is £1,203,912, and the instalments issued amount to £1,032,132.

The number of applications for loans lodged during the year 1898–99 was 938, being an increase of 141 over last year. Of this number 65 were received from occupying owners, who were prevented by some feature in their application from proceeding under the Land Improvement Act.

The following table gives the distribution by Counties of the sums issued for all classes of work under the 31st Section of the Land Law (Ireland) Act, 1881, from the passing of the Act:—

SCHEDULE showing the NUMBER of LOANS SANCTIONED and AMOUNTS ISSUED up to the 31st MARCH, 1899.

Provinces and Counties.	Number of Loans Sanctioned.			Amounts Sanctioned.			Total Issued.		
	To 31st Mar., 1898.	Year ending 31st Mar., 1899.	Total Number.	To 31st Mar., 1898.	Year ending 31st Mar., 1899.	Total Sanctioned.	To 31st Mar., 1898.	Year ending 31st Mar., 1899.	Total Issued.
LEINSTER:				£	£	£	£	£	£
Carlow, . .	100	9	109	13,615	750	14,365	9,371	852	10,223
Dublin, . .	185	10	195	25,310	950	26,260	23,010	1,307	24,317
Kildare, . .	197	6	203	22,045	645	22,690	22,113	491	22,604
Kilkenny, . .	238	35	273	30,675	1,085	31,760	17,304	1,228	18,532
King's, . .	232	11	243	22,725	965	23,690	17,356	706	18,062
Longford, . .	315	–	315	26,175	–	26,175	24,601	173	24,774
Louth, . .	73	3	76	8,495	115	8,610	6,317	38	6,355
Meath, . .	262	13	275	36,973	3,165	40,138	33,783	1,790	35,573
Queen's, . .	157	15	172	14,730	1,450	16,180	11,664	690	12,354
Westmeath, . .	308	17	325	32,610	2,125	34,735	27,321	1,210	28,531
Wexford, . .	165	15	180	16,670	983	17,653	14,744	1,150	15,894
Wicklow, . .	163	12	175	17,505	1,110	18,615	14,183	1,270	15,474
Totals, . .	2,445	143	2,588	287,300	12,223	299,523	236,555	11,376	247,931
MUNSTER:									
Clare, . .	763	17	780	60,393	1,060	61,453	32,259	817	33,076
Cork, . .	2,341	105	2,446	201,125	8,015	209,140	175,227	6,943	182,170
Kerry, . .	1,030	71	1,101	78,560	3,915	82,475	63,150	2,290	65,395
Limerick, . .	884	96	980	78,787	7,016	85,803	68,249	3,867	71,114
Tipperary, . .	848	107	955	73,541	6,490	79,035	62,741	5,316	68,057
Waterford, . .	127	16	143	11,710	1,540	13,250	9,152	1,471	10,623
Totals, . .	5,995	414	6,409	503,050	28,096	531,646	460,603	23,814	484,417
ULSTER:									
Antrim, . .	129	1	130	12,575	67	12,642	11,109	184	11,293
Armagh, . .	99	–	99	8,485	–	8,485	8,125	78	8,203
Cavan, . .	669	13	682	48,115	610	48,725	38,120	842	38,962
Donegal, . .	374	3	377	19,917	161	20,078	17,073	157	17,230
Down, . .	88	10	98	8,875	935	9,810	7,773	740	8,513
Fermanagh, . .	171	5	176	11,355	600	11,955	9,128	–	9,128
Londonderry, . .	139	2	141	11,073	190	11,263	9,877	246	10,123
Monaghan, . .	106	5	111	8,080	305	8,385	8,582	192	8,774
Tyrone, . .	245	8	253	22,081	400	22,481	16,434	141	16,575
Totals, . .	1,944	46	1,990	144,182	3,265	147,447	122,292	2,577	124,869
CONNAUGHT:									
Galway, . .	636	14	650	51,533	780	52,313	44,772	636	45,408
Leitrim, . .	612	9	621	36,780	175	36,955	34,760	123	34,883
Mayo, . .	975	8	983	72,115	185	72,300	62,178	815	62,993
Roscommon, . .	354	8	362	42,870	1,010	43,880	36,162	467	36,629
Sligo, . .	283	1	284	37,553	50	37,603	33,821	114	33,935
Totals, . .	2,860	40	2,900	240,851	2,200	243,051	211,693	2,155	213,848
Grand Totals,	13,244	643	13,887	1,175,383	45,784	1,221,667	1,031,143	39,922	1,071,065

In the Report for 1894–5 the total number of loans sanctioned for Co. Roscommon is shown as 259, whereas the correct number should have been 255; and in the Report for 1895–6 the number of loans sanctioned for Co. Wexford is given as 265, whereas the correct number is 165. These inaccuracies have been corrected in the above table.

We submit a statement classifying the loans in which works have been completed under the different descriptions of work, to the 31st March, 1899:—

Description of Work.	Amounts Expended		
	From passing of Act to 31st March, 1898.	For year ending 31st March, 1899.	Total from passing of Act to 31st March, 1899.
	£ s. d.	£ s. d.	£ s. d.
Drainage, Fencing, Farm Roads, and other Land Works,	420,015 11 9	3,464 10 6	423,480 11 3
Farm Houses and Offices,	569,477 12 11	37,458 6 4	606,935 16 3
Labourers' Cottages, 19th section,	10,152 18 10	Nil.	10,159 18 10
Labourers' Cottages, 31st section,	14,424 8 2	Nil.	14,421 8 3
Scutch Mills for Flax,	926 13 6	Nil.	926 15 6
	1,019,169 0 3	40,822 3 10	1,060,691 3 1

The number of loans in which the amounts sanctioned have been expended and the works certified as completed, is 12,144, and those in which the works were still in progress on the 31st March, 1899, is 442.

CLASS (4).—MISCELLANEOUS LOANS.

Glebe Loans. No. 81 in Abstract, p. 56.

Forty-one applications for loans, amounting to £14,455, have been received during the year, and 40 loans, for £16,316, have been sanctioned. The applications show an increase of 5, and the sanctions an increase of 9, representing £4,926, over the corresponding figures for the previous period. The issues for the year amounted to £14,536. Since the passing of the first Act, in 1870, we have received 1,688 applications, of which the following is an abstract of those on which issues were made to the 31st March, 1899:—

Denomination.	No.	Amount.
		£
Roman Catholic,	772	310,187
Church of Ireland,	296	139,304
Presbyterian,	216	70,474
Wesleyan and others,	86	27,027
	1,370	576,139

Loans for National School Teachers' Residences. No. 87 in Abstract, p. 56.

Forty-four applications for loans, amounting to £9,186, have been received during the year, and 41 loans, including some applied for in the previous year, have been sanctioned, for £9,973. The applications show a falling-off of 9 as compared with last year, while the sanctions show an increase of 3 in number and of £1,896 in amount. The amount actually advanced in the year was £7,949. The total advances for loans of this class from the passing of the Act to the date above-named amounted to £192,932 10s.; the total number of loans sanctioned is 938.

Loans for National Schools and Training Colleges. No. 88 in Abstract, p. 56.

Eight applications for loans for National Schools, amounting to £2,277, have been received during the year, as against three applications for £890 during the year 1897-98. The number of loans sanctioned in the year was 4, and the amount £1,942. Two large loans for Training Colleges have been made during the year, namely, one of £16,000 for a college for the training of female teachers in Limerick, and the second of £12,000 for a similar institution in Belfast.

IRISH CHURCH FUND LOANS.

No loans or advances under previous loans were made from this fund during the year.

Out of £1,269,983 advanced from the Irish Church Fund under the Relief of Distress Act of 1880, £716,227 has been repaid, £33,315 has been remitted, and of the balance outstanding, £520,390, £505,781 is not yet due, £6,123 is regarded as irrecoverable, and £8,486 is in arrear.

The rate of interest on these loans is 1 per cent., but borrowers paying land improvement and arterial drainage charges, are allowed to redeem their principal liabilities on the basis of 3 per cent. interest. The principal cancelled by such redemptions now amounts to £14,240, including £1,282 in the present year.

RATES OF INTEREST.

The following statement shows the rates of interest chargeable on the several amounts, making the aggregate balances in each year ended 31st March, 1897, 1898, and 1899, respectively :—

—	31 March, 1897.	31 March, 1898.	31 March, 1899.
	£	£	£
Free of Interest,	11,404	10,913	10,490
2½ per cent.,	—	68,710	198,442
3 "	6,000	13,970	35,795
3⅛ "	1,316,737	1,238,330	1,198,125
3¼ "	747,283	761,906	814,975
3⅜ "	189,082	208,784	208,345
3½ "	3,303,090	4,538,301	3,727,834
3¾ "	830,190	823,976	808,072
4 "	1,345,380	1,071,161	1,025,823
4½ "	208,176	161,732	155,447
5 "	38,607	85,580	33,378
Advances on which interest is deferred, pending the completion of the works.	1,270	8,161	3,199
Total Local Loans Fund,	7,689,537	7,916,483	8,238,276
Church Fund Loans— at 1 per cent.,	587,108	549,779	514,787
	*8,276,645	†8,466,262	‡8,753,063

* Exclusive of { £301,170 written off from the Account of the Assets of the Local Loans Fund. £5,763 portion of Church Fund Loans, considered as irrecoverable.

† " { £306,078 written off from the Account of the Assets of the Local Loans Fund. £3,765 portion of Church Fund Loans, considered as irrecoverable.

‡ " { £307,438 written off from the Account of the Assets of the Local Loans Fund. £6,123 portion of Church Fund Loans, considered as irrecoverable.

The average rate chargeable on the advances out of the Local Loans Fund was £3 10s. 9d. on the 31st March, 1897; £3 10s. 4d. on the 31st March, 1898; and £3 10s. on the 31st March, 1899. The interest realised in the year averaged £3 7s. 10d. per cent. on the principal sum outstanding on the 1st April, 1898.

[illegible]

Month	[illegible]
April	[illegible]
May	[illegible]
June	[illegible]
July	[illegible]
August	[illegible]
September	[illegible]
October	[illegible]
November	[illegible]
December	[illegible]
January, 1859	[illegible]
February	[illegible]
March	[illegible]
Total	[illegible]

KINGSTOWN HARBOUR—*Annual Return of Fish.*

Month.	Hampers.	Amount.			Remarks.
		£	s.	d.	
April,	384	384	0	0	Trawlers employed, 37; the fishing has fallen off considerably; the fishermen attribute it to the number of steam trawlers at work.
May,	318	318	0	0	
June,	341	364	0	0	
July,	300	353	0	0	
August,	331	328	0	0	
September,	678	670	0	0	
October,	377	381	0	0	Local line fishing has been good; herring and mackerel fishing bad; lobsters and crabs none; prawns fairly numerous.
November,	371	381	0	0	
December,	463	499	0	0	
January,	373	373	0	0	
February,	169	169	0	0	
March,	184	184	0	0	
Total,	4,184	4,410	0	0	

HOWTH HARBOUR.

Imports.—Dressed stone, 80 tons; coal, 6,846 tons, a decrease of 763 tons on the coal imported for the year ending 31st March, 1898. Exports, nil.

The hook line fishing has been fairly maintained for the greater part of the year, and many first-class boats continue to be employed in it. The total quantity of line fish caught was 9,397 cleeves, a decrease of 4,693 cleeves on the quantity caught for the year ending 31st March, 1898. The amount realised was £7,460 1s., an average of 15s. 8½d. per cleeve.

The herring fishery shows a marked improvement on many past years. Several Cornish, Scotch, and Manx, as well as local boats, were engaged in it. The total quantity caught was 3,947 mease, against 177 mease for the previous year. The price realised was £2,691 8s., being an average of 13s. 4½d. per mease.

The total amount realised for fish sold was:—

	£	s.	d.
Hooked Fish,	7,460	1	0
Herrings,	2,691	8	0
	£10,151	9	0

The harbour continues to be used as a port of refuge during winter by Ringsend trawlers, and by vessels seeking shelter and waiting for tides to get into Malahide and Rogerstown.

DUNMORE EAST HARBOUR.

Import of coal, 1,552 tons—a decrease of 108 tons on last year's import.

Import of salt, 768 tons—an increase (attributable to a successful herring fishing) of 397 tons over last year's import.

Exports.—Herrings, 82,319 mease; average price, 8s. 7d. per mease; total price, £5,893 10s. 6d.; trawl fish, 445 cwt.; average price, 14s. 8d. per cwt.; total price, £326 5s. 6d.; lobsters, 720 doz.; average price, 7s. 6d. per doz.; total price, £270; crabs, 500 doz.; average price, 2s. per doz.; total price, £50.

The autumn herring fishing (from the last week of July to the 17th December) was most successful. The quantity captured was 83,949 mease, showing an increase over the previous year of 10,593 mease. Of this, 1,480 mease remained unsold.

Shell fishers here did well in the earlier part of the season. They followed the herring fishing in the later months.

Shipping entering the harbour to discharge or load—33 vessels, 1,845 tons, 154 men. Cargo vessels entering the harbour for shelter—1 vessel, 84 tons, 7 men.

Fishing boats employed fishing off the harbour—7 Scotch, 64 Irish; total, 71; 504 men, 56 boys. Fishing boats using the harbour for shelter—Cornish, 1; Scotch, 7; Manx, 14; Irish, 29; total 51; 348 men, 50 boys. Tug-boats and yachts putting in for shelter—Tug-boats, 8; yachts, 17.

Donaghadee Harbour.

A Return showing the Harbour Service for the Twelve Months ending the 31st March, 1899.

Return of Imports.

Months.	[illegible]	Cargo.	[illegible]	[illegible]	[illegible]	Cargo.	[illegible]	[illegible]	[illegible]	Cargo.	[illegible]	[illegible]	[illegible]	Cargo.	[illegible]	[illegible]	[illegible]	[illegible]	[illegible]	[illegible]
1898.																				
April,	5	Coals.	[illegible]	[illegible]	1	Maize,	[illegible]	[illegible]	–	.	–	–	–	.	–	–	–	–	–	[illegible]
May,	[illegible]	"	[illegible]	[illegible]	–	–	–	–	–	.	–	–	–	.	–	–	–	–	–	[illegible]
June,	5	"	[illegible]	[illegible]	–	–	–	–	–	–	–	–	–	.	–	–	–	–	–	[illegible]
July,	[illegible]	"	771	[illegible]	1	Maize,	[illegible]	[illegible]	1	Gravel,	[illegible]	[illegible]	–	–	–	–	–	–	–	[illegible]
August,	[illegible]	"	[illegible]	[illegible]	–	–	–	–	1	.	[illegible]	[illegible]	–	–	–	–	–	–	–	[illegible]
September,	[illegible]	"	[illegible]	[illegible]	–	–	–	–	–	.	–	–	–	–	–	–	–	–	–	[illegible]
October,	[illegible]	"	[illegible]	[illegible]	–	–	–	–	–	.	–	–	–	–	–	–	–	–	–	[illegible]
November,	[illegible]	"	[illegible]	[illegible]	[illegible]	Maize,	[illegible]	[illegible]	–	–	–	–	–	–	–	–	–	–	–	[illegible]
December,	[illegible]	"	[illegible]	[illegible]	[illegible]	"	[illegible]	[illegible]	–	–	–	–	–	–	–	–	–	–	–	[illegible]
1899.																				
January,	7	–	[illegible]	[illegible]	–	–	–	–	–	–	–	–	–	–	–	–	–	–	–	[illegible]
February,	[illegible]	"	[illegible]	[illegible]	[illegible]	Maize,	[illegible]	[illegible]	–	–	–	–	–	–	–	–	–	–	–	[illegible]
March,	[illegible]	"	[illegible]	[illegible]	1	"	[illegible]	[illegible]	–	–	–	–	–	–	–	–	–	–	–	[illegible]
	[illegible]	"	[illegible]	[illegible]	9	Maize,	[illegible]	[illegible]	[illegible]	Gravel,	[illegible]	[illegible]	–	–	–	–	–	–	–	[illegible]

Return of Exports.

—	No. of Tons.
Scrap Iron,	77
Brick,	236

Vessels resorting to the Harbour for Shelter.

No. of Vessels.	No. of Tons Register.	Fishing Vessels.	No. of Tons Register.	Number of Men.
79	[illegible]	[illegible]	[illegible]	[illegible]

Other Vessels using the Harbour.

Tugboats.	Yachts.
41	46

The correct number of boats or yawls that fished out of the harbour for the past year, 906; number of fish, 4,593 score; the amount of money, £473 15s. 8d.

The Belfast and County Down Railways steam boats made about 77 calls, and landed on pier head about 6,000 passengers, and took about the same number from the pier head.

Ardglass Harbour.

The herring fishing commenced here on the 25th May, and continued up to the 10th September. The total capture for the year was 8,667 mease, an increase of 6,977 mease over the previous year. The estimated amount realised was £3,820 19s. 6d. The average price per mease was 8s. 9½d. The boats fishing from the harbour numbered 15 Scotch, 2 Manx, and 38 Irish, in all 55 boats—10 less than the total for the last year. The capture of herrings was about 157½ mease per boat during the season, lasting 108 days, against 23 mease per boat for the previous season, lasting 55 days.

During the time of herring fishing the capture of mackerel was 198 mease; estimated amount realised, £128 3s. 6d. The prices obtained varied from 6s. 6d. down to 1s. per hundred. Hand fishing was carried on by 6 yawls at all seasonable times, but owing to the great scarcity of fish, and the unsettled state of the weather through the winter, this class of fishing was not successful. Only one of the larger herring boats belonging to this district was engaged trawling after the herring season. The quantity of fish captured was small. The fishermen still complain of the injury done by steam trawlers. The total quantity of mixed fish sold at this port during the year was 211 tons (90½ tons less than that sold in the previous year), and the estimated amount realised, £187 17s. 6d. (£377 19s. less than previous year).

The shipping of all kinds to and from the port was as follows:—

Nine steamers, registered tonnage 546, arrived and discharged .	1,200 tons coal (imported).
Six steamers, registered tonnage 423, arrived and shipped . .	1,016 tons potatoes.
Three sailing vessels, registered tonnage 180, arrived and shipped .	270 ,, ,,
Six pleasure steamers, registered tonnage 591, from Belfast and back with passengers. These vessels imported	45 tons manure and sundries.
Total tonnage of merchandise by above vessels, . . .	2,531

In addition to the above, 2 tug steamers and 1 steamship called for shelter or for orders, and 4 sailing vessels for shelter; also a number of fishing boats from Scotland coming to and returning from the South and West of Ireland fishing grounds, &c.

The shipping trade was better than in the previous year. The coal import was less by 200 tons, but this was more than counterbalanced by the increase (787 tons) in the export of potatoes.

APPENDIX (D 1).

National and Ancient Monuments.

Irish Church, 1869, 32 & 33 Vic., c. 42; Ancient Monuments Protection Act, 1882, 45 & 46 Vic., c. 73; Ancient Monuments Protection Act, 1892, 55 & 56 Vic., c. 46.

A List of Ruins that came under consideration during the year is given under five heads:—

1. Ruins recommended to the Board for vesting.
2. Ruins in course of vesting.
3. Ruins vested.
4. Ruins vested and awaiting repairs.
5. Ruins repaired.

1. Ruins recommended for vesting—

Arboe Cross, Cookstown, .	Co. Tyrone.
Ferns Castle, . . .	Co. Wexford.
Fore Abbey, . . .	Co. Westmeath.
Galbally, . . .	Co. Tipperary.

2. Ruins in course of vesting—

Clonmines (Cowboys' Chapel), . . Co. Wexford.

3. Ruins vested—

Duleek Priory, ... Co. Meath.

4. Ruins vested and awaiting repair—

Clare Galway Abbey, . . . Co. Galway.
Canons' Island, ... Co. Clare.
Hospital Old Church, . . . Co. Limerick.

5. Ruins repaired—

Clare Abbey, ... Co. Clare.
New Grange, ... Co. Meath.
Dingle Promontory, . . . Co. Kerry.
Dowth Moat, ... Co. Meath.
Donegal Castle, ... Co. Donegal.
Donegal Abbey, ... Co. Donegal.
Kells Abbey, ... Co. Kilkenny.
St. Columb's House, Kells, . . Co. Meath.
Bective Abbey, ... Co. Meath.

The following are the principal works of repair carried out during the year:—

1. *Clare Abbey.*—Vested in 1896. The work here consisted of pointing the north wall, rebuilding the inside jambs and arches to door opes, and strengthening the masonry about them; underpinning, where necessary; and repairing the parapet of the tower and embrasures. Iron window guards were provided, and the gates secured.

2. *Donegal Abbey.*—Vested in 1898. The cloisters were repaired, and the walls pointed and concreted on the top. Underpinning was also carried out.

3. *Kells Abbey.*—Extensive repairs to masonry were executed at this monument, which was vested in 1893. The monument is ecclesiastical so far as regards the Abbey, and partly non-ecclesiastical, a portion of the ruins consisting of fortifications. The repairs of the Abbey have been met out of the National Monuments Fund, and those of the fortifications out of the provision in the Votes for Ancient Monuments.

4. *Donegal Castle.*—Vested in 1898. The walls were carefully pointed and the masonry repaired and secured. Considerable underpinning was carried out. The tops of the walls were concreted, and the gates and windows made secure.

APPENDIX R.—STATEMENT showing the Loans made by the Board of Works to Aid in the Construction of Railways under the Act 1 & 2 Wm. IV., cap. 33.

Railway.	Amount Advanced. £ s. d.	Principal Outstanding, 31st March, 1898. £ s. d.	Principal Outstanding, 31st March, 1899. £ s. d.	Remarks.
Ballymena, Cushendall and Red Bay Railway.	37,700 0 0	—	—	
Ballycastle,	30,000 0 0	—	—	Board's interest sold. Balance remitted by Public Works Loans Act, 1897.
Ballymena and Larne,	44,350 0 0	—	—	
Clara and Banagher,	(a) 30,000 0 0	—	—	(a) The purchase of the line by the Great Southern and Western Company was completed during the year 1896–7. The balance outstanding, £23,000, was remitted by the Public Works Loans Act, 1897.
	(b) 35,346 0 0	23,187 1 9	22,680 11 0	
Clonakilty Extension,	30,000 0 0	—	—	
Cork and Bandon (Bantry Extension).	25,000 0 0	—	—	(b) The repayment of this loan is guaranteed by the Barony of Garrycastle, King's County, under the Relief of Distress Amendment Act, 1880.
Dublin to Kingstown,	112,300 0 0	—	—	
	36,000 0 0	—	—	
Dublin and Lucan,	10,000 0 0	—	—	
Derry Central,	100,000 0 0	100,000 0 0	100,000 0 0	
Donegal,	(c) 40,000 0 0	—	—	(c) For West Donegal Line.
	13,500 0 0	—	—	
Draperstown,	14,000 0 0	—	—	
Giant's Causeway, Portrush and Bush Valley.	(d) 10,000 0 0	—	—	(d) The Board's charge has been assigned and the purchase money, £6,000, was lodged in May, 1897. The balance, £3,972, was remitted by the Public Works Loans Act, 1897.
Ilen Valley,	40,000 0 0	—	—	
Limavady and Dungiven,	19,601 0 0	19,601 0 0	19,601 0 0	
Letterkenny,	60,000 0 0	60,000 0 0	60,000 0 0	
	(e) 28,000 0 0	28,234 1 2	27,287 3 3	(e) The repayment of this Loan was guaranteed by certain Baronies in the Counties of Donegal and Londonderry under the Relief of Distress Amendment Act, 1880.
Sligo, Leitrim, and Northern Counties.	98,622 0 0	49,375 0 0	48,875 0 0	
Sligo and Ballaghaderreen,	12,880 0 0	—	—	
Southern,	86,164 17 5	86,164 17 5	86,164 17 5	
Ulster,	70,000 0 0	—	—	
Waterford, Dungarvan, and Lismore.	(f) 93,570 16 8	83,980 16 5	83,880 16 8	(f) See special par., p. 23.
Waterford and Wexford,	(g) 43,000 0 0	43,000 0 0	43,000 0 0	(g) This line has been transferred to the Fishguard and Rosslare Railways and Harbours Co., and £38,000 of the advance has been written off from the Assets of the Local Loans Fund.
Cavan, Leitrim, and Roscommon.	68,000 0 0	—	—	These Loans were made on the security of Baronial guaranteed shares, under the Public Works Loans (Tramways Ireland) Act, 1886, 49 & 50 Vic., c. 16.
Clogher Valley,	44,000 0 0	—	—	
Cork and Muskerry,	18,700 0 0	—	—	
Donegal (West Donegal Light Railway).	(h) 7,000 0 0	6,439 13 3	—	
West Clare,	84,400 0 0	—	—	(h) The Treasury liability was redeemed in July, 1898, and the Loan repaid with the funds then provided.
	1,300,137 14 1	479,623 10 9	472,909 7 3	

NOTE.—The rate of Interest chargeable up to the 30th of June, 1898, was 4 per cent.; [illegible]

The following is an ABSTRACT of LOANS made by the COMMISSIONERS of PUBLIC WORKS, showing the Amounts Remitted, and

No.	Acts under which Advances made.	PURPOSES FOR WHICH ADVANCED.	No. of Loans [illegible]	Advanced for these purposes. In the Year ended 31st March, 18[illegible].	Advanced for these purposes. Total up to the 31st March, 18[illegible].	PRINCIPAL. In the Year ended [illegible] Principal.
	a.	b.	c.	d.	e.	f.
		I. Public Works Loans, 1 & 2 Wm. IV., c. 33, and 40 & 41 Vic., c. 71.				
		CLASS I.—LOANS SECURED ON UNDERTAKINGS.		£ s. d.	£ s. d.	£ s. d.
1	1 & 2 Wm. IV., c. 33,	Local Boards—various works,	17	1,[illegible] [illegible] [illegible]	165,[illegible] [illegible] [illegible]	[illegible]
2	Do.	Inland Navigation,	[illegible]	—	1[illegible] [illegible] [illegible]	[illegible]
3	Do.	Railways,	10	—	1,[illegible],127 [illegible] [illegible]	[illegible]
4	Do.	Quarries, Mines, &c.,	4	10,[illegible] [illegible] [illegible]	[illegible]	[illegible]
5	Do.	Harbours, Docks, &c.,	[illegible]	[illegible]	[illegible]	[illegible]
6	Do.	Reclamation of Waste Lands,	—	—	[illegible]	—
7	[illegible] Vic., c. [illegible]	Labourers' Dwellings in Towns,	74	—	[illegible]	(a) 1,[illegible]
8	[illegible] Vic., c. [illegible]; and [illegible] Vic., c. 70.	Housing of the Working Classes,	[illegible]	[illegible]	[illegible]	[illegible]
			[illegible]	[illegible]	[illegible]	[illegible]
		CLASS II.—LOANS SECURED ON RATES.				
9	1 & 2 Wm. IV., c. 33,	Grand Juries of Counties for Roads, Court Houses, &c.,	[illegible]	[illegible]	[illegible]	[illegible]
10	Do.	Roads and Bridges,	[illegible]	—	[illegible]	[illegible]
11	[illegible] Vic., cc. [illegible]; [illegible] Vic., c. [illegible]; [illegible] Vic., c. [illegible]	Public Buildings; Public Libraries; Reformatories; and Industrial Schools,	[illegible]	—	[illegible]	[illegible]
12	[illegible] Vic., c. [illegible]	Fishery Piers and Harbours,	—	—	[illegible]	—
13	57 Geo. III., c. [illegible]	Public Works Loans,	[illegible]	—	[illegible]	—
14	[illegible] Wm. IV., c. [illegible]	Repairs of Post Roads and Bridges,	[illegible]	[illegible]	[illegible]	[illegible]
15	[illegible] Vic., c. [illegible]	Repairs of Fishery Piers and Harbours,	[illegible]	[illegible]	[illegible]	—
16	[illegible] Vic., c. [illegible]	Maintenance of Navigation Works,	—	—	2,[illegible]	—
17	[illegible] Geo. IV., c. [illegible]; [illegible] Vic., c. [illegible]	Lunatic Asylums Buildings,	[illegible]	[illegible]	[illegible]	[illegible]
18	[illegible] Vic., c. [illegible]	Artisans' Dwellings,	1	—	[illegible]	[illegible]
19	[illegible] Vic., c. [illegible]; [illegible] Vic., c. [illegible]	Public Health,	[illegible]	[illegible]	[illegible]	[illegible]
20	[illegible] Vic., c. 17,	Emigration,	[illegible]	—	11,[illegible]	[illegible]
21	[illegible] Vic., c. [illegible]; [illegible] Vic., c. 77.	Labourers' Acts,	[illegible]	[illegible]	1,[illegible]	[illegible]
22	[illegible] Vic., c. [illegible]	Dispensary Houses,	[illegible]	[illegible]	[illegible]	2,[illegible]
23	[illegible] Vic., c. [illegible], sch. [illegible]	Workhouse Buildings, &c.,	[illegible]	[illegible]	[illegible]	—
			[illegible]	[illegible]	[illegible]	[illegible]
		CLASS III.—LOANS SECURED ON LANDS.				
24	[illegible] Vic., c. [illegible]	River Drainage and Navigation,	[illegible]	—	[illegible]	—
25	[illegible] Vic., c. [illegible]	River Drainage,	[illegible]	[illegible]	[illegible]	[illegible]
26	[illegible] Vic., c. [illegible]	River Drainage Maintenance,	[illegible]	—	[illegible]	[illegible]
		(Continued on next page.)				

...Advances and Repayments in the Year, the Total Advances and Repayments to the 31st March, 1899, the ... the Balances Outstanding.

... and INTEREST paid by Borrowers.			Remitted.	PRINCIPAL Outstanding against Borrowers on 31st March, 1899.				No.
... March, 1899.	Total to 31st March, 1899.			Principal.			Interest.	
				In Arrear.		Not yet due.		
Interest.	Principal.	Interest.		Written off from the Account of ...	Other Arrears.			
£ s. d.	£ s. d.	£ s. d.	£ s. d.	£ s. d.	£ s. d.	£ s. d.	£ s. d.	
[illegible]	[illegible]	[illegible]	—	—	—	[illegible]	—	1
[illegible]	[illegible]	[illegible]	[illegible]	[illegible]	—	[illegible]	—	2
[illegible]	[illegible]	[illegible]	[illegible]	[illegible]	[illegible]	[illegible]	[illegible]	3
[illegible]	[illegible]	[illegible]	—	—	—	[illegible]	—	4
[illegible]	[illegible]	[illegible]	[illegible]	—	[illegible]	[illegible]	[illegible]	5
—	[illegible]	[illegible]	—	[illegible]	—	—	—	6
[illegible]	[illegible]	[illegible]	[illegible]	[illegible]	[illegible]	[illegible]	[illegible]	7
[illegible]	[illegible]	[illegible]	—	—	[illegible]	[illegible]	[illegible]	8
[illegible]	[illegible]	[illegible]	[illegible]	[illegible]	[illegible]	[illegible]	[illegible]	
[illegible]	[illegible]	[illegible]	—	—	—	[illegible]	—	9
[illegible]	[illegible]	[illegible]	[illegible]	—	—	[illegible]	—	10
[illegible]	[illegible]	[illegible]	[illegible]	—	[illegible]	[illegible]	[illegible]	11

The following is an Abstract of Loans made by the Commissioners of Public Works, showing the Amounts remitted, and

No.	Acts under which Advances have been made.	Purposes for which advanced.	No. of each Loan ... 31st March, 1899.	Advanced to Borrowers. In the Year ended 31st March, 1899.	Total up to the 31st March, 1899.	Principal. In the Year ended ... Principal.
	a.	b.	c.	d.	e.	f.
		CLASS III.—continued.		£ s. d.	£ s. d.	£ s. d.
27	[illegible]	Improvement of Lands—viz., Drainage, Erection of Farm Buildings and Farm Labourers' Dwellings, Planting for Shelter,	[illegible]	[illegible] 0 0	[illegible]	[illegible]
28	[illegible]	Land Improvement Preliminary Expenses,	1	[illegible] 0 0	[illegible] 0 0	[illegible]
29	[illegible]	Land Law—Advances to Occupiers of Land for Improvement of their Holdings.	[illegible]	[illegible] 0 0	[illegible] 0 0	[illegible]
30	[illegible]	For Advances to Tenants for Purchase of their Farms, &c.,	[illegible]	—	[illegible]	[illegible]
			[illegible]	[illegible] 0 0	[illegible]	[illegible]
		CLASS IV.—Miscellaneous Loans.				
31	[illegible]	Glebe Loans,	[illegible]	[illegible] 0 0	[illegible]	[illegible]
32	[illegible]	Building Schools,	1	—	[illegible]	[illegible]
33	[illegible]	Seed Supply,	[illegible]	—	[illegible]	[illegible]
34	[illegible]	Do.,	[illegible]	—	[illegible]	—
35	[illegible]	Do.,	7	—	[illegible] 0 0	[illegible]
36	[illegible]	Do.,	[illegible]	[illegible]	[illegible]	[illegible]
37	[illegible]	National School Teachers' Residences,	[illegible]	[illegible] 0 0	[illegible]	[illegible]
38	[illegible]	Non-Vested Schools and Training Colleges,	[illegible]	[illegible] 0 0	[illegible]	[illegible]
			[illegible]	[illegible]	[illegible]	[illegible]
		Total Current and Unfunded Services,	[illegible]	[illegible]	[illegible]	[illegible]
		Add Total Closed Services,	—	—	[illegible]	—
		Gross Total Local Loans Fund,	[illegible]	[illegible]	[illegible]	[illegible]
		II. Irish Church Fund Loans.				
		CLASS II.—Loans secured on Rates.				
39	[illegible]	Public Health,	[illegible]	—	[illegible]	[illegible]
40	Do.,	Baronial Works,	[illegible]	—	[illegible]	[illegible]
41	Do.,	Relief of Distress,	—	—	[illegible]	..
42	Do.,	Relief of Distress Grants,	—	—	[illegible]	—
			[illegible]	—	[illegible]	[illegible]
		CLASS III.—Loans secured on Lands.				
43	Do.,	Improvement of Lands,	[illegible]	—	[illegible]	[illegible]
44	Do.	Arterial Drainage,	[illegible]	—	[illegible]	[illegible]
			[illegible]	—	[illegible]	[illegible]
		Total Irish Church Fund Loans,	[illegible]	—	[illegible]	[illegible]
		Grand Total,	[illegible]	[illegible]	[illegible]	[illegible]

Advances and Repayments in the Year, the Total Advances and Repayments to the 31st March, 1859, the [illegible] Balances Outstanding—continued.

[illegible] and INTEREST paid by Borrowers			Remitted.	BALANCES Outstanding against Borrowers on 31st March, 1859.				No.
[illegible] March, 1859.	Paid to 31st March, 1859.			Principal.			Interest.	
				In Arrear.		Not yet due.		
Interest.	Principal.	Interest.		[illegible]	Other Amounts.			
g.	h.	i.	k.	l.	m.	n.	o.	
£ s. d.	£ s. d.	£ s. d.	£ s. d.	£ s. d.	£ s. d.	£ s. d.	£ s. d.	
[illegible]	[illegible]	[illegible]	—	[illegible]	[illegible]	[illegible]	[illegible]	[illegible]
—	[illegible]	—	[illegible]	[illegible]	—	[illegible]	—	[illegible]
[illegible]	[illegible]	[illegible]	—	[illegible]	[illegible]	[illegible]	[illegible]	[illegible]
[illegible]	[illegible]	[illegible]	—	[illegible]	[illegible]	[illegible]	[illegible]	[illegible]
[illegible]	[illegible]	[illegible]	[illegible]	[illegible]	[illegible]	[illegible]	[illegible]	
[illegible]	[illegible]	[illegible]	—	—	[illegible]	[illegible]	[illegible]	[illegible]
[illegible]	[illegible]	[illegible]	[illegible]	—	—	[illegible]	—	[illegible]
—	[illegible]	[illegible]	—	—	[illegible]	—	—	[illegible]
[illegible]	[illegible]	[illegible]	—	—	[illegible]	—	—	[illegible]
[illegible]	[illegible]	[illegible]	—	—	[illegible]	—	—	[illegible]

APPENDIX G.—

(G.)—ABSTRACT of the ACCOUNTS of the COMMISSIONERS of PUBLIC WORKS in IRELAND, showing the Total of

No. of Account.	Page.	Heads of Account.	Balance on 31st March, 1898.	Receipts.
			£ s. d.	£ s. d.
G 1	64–69	Parliamentary Votes and Grants, viz. :— 1. Public Works and Buildings, Ireland, 2. Railways (Ireland) Acts, 1889, 1890, and 1896, 3. Light Railways (Ireland), Act, 1889 (Non-Voted Advances), 4. Tramways Act, 1883 do., 5. Railways Act, 1896 do., 6. Public Works Office, Ireland, 7. Adjustments affecting the Votes for 1897, 1898,	16,437 17 10	[illegible] 14 5
G 2	70–71	Loans Advanced,	93,[illegible] 11 4	[illegible] 9 5
G 3	72–73	Loans Repayments,	—	[illegible] 1 1
G 4	72–73	Land Improvement Preliminaries, 10 Vic., c. 32,	—	[illegible] 1 1
G 5	74–75	District Lunatic Asylums,	21,842 6 7	[illegible] 13 1
G 6	74–75	Sea Fisheries, Ireland, 16 & 17 Vic., c. [illegible],	12,287 6 6	3,163 16 1
G 7	76–81	Miscellaneous Services, viz. :— 1. Deposit Accounts, 1 & 2 Wm. IV., c. 33, &c., 2. Railway and other Arbitrations, 14 & 15 Vic., c. 70, 3. Arterial Drainage Deposits, 26 & 27 Vic., c. 88, &c., 4. Fees—Inquiries, 16 & 17 Vic., c. 136, 5. Inland Navigations.—Shannon, 6. Drainage Maintenance, 29 & 30 Vic., c. 49, 7. National Monuments, 32 & 33 Vic., c. 42, 8. Sea and Coast Fisheries Loan Fund, 47 & 48 Vic., c. 21, &c., 9. Linen Hall, 10. Galway Harbour Receiver's Account, 11. Southern Railway, 12. Letterkenny Railway, 13. Sundry Accounts,	6,[illegible] 7 1	[illegible]
		Total,	81,[illegible]	[illegible]
G 8	82–87	Statement of Final Awards under Arterial Drainage Act, 26 & 27 Vic., c. 88, with Repayments thereon, to the 31st March, 1899.		

ACCOUNTS.

Sums intrusted to their Management for Collection or Disbursement for Year ended 31st March, 1879.

[illegible]	Totals.	[illegible]	Paid.	[illegible]	Totals.
£ s. d.	£ s. d.	£ s. d.	£ s. d.	£ s. d.	£ s. d.
—	476,869 14 9	—	447,096 1 9	29,629 10 6	476,665 11 3
—	673,946 11 4	—	662,790 5 5	10,156 6 1	672,946 11 4
—	846,761 4 8	—	813,761 4 8	—	845,761 4 6
4 6 4	3,009 5 10	—	3,138 11 10	146 11 9	3,335 3 10
—	766,271 14 11	—	650,705 7 6	15,563 11 5	766,271 14 11
—	16,411 8 11	—	300 2 4	16,031 1 7	16,411 8 11
—	41,161 16 3	—	34,162 10 0	7,078 19 2	41,161 16 3
4 6 4	2,194,064 4 5	—	2,080,676 4 3	72,896 10 11	2,154,064 4 5

An Account showing the Receipts and Expenditure of the Com[missioners]

(G 1.)—PARLIAMENTARY

RECEIPTS.	£ s. d.	£ s. d.	£ s. d.
Balance from last Account,	—	—	16,487 17 10
Public Works and Buildings.—Class I. Vote 13.			
Vote for the year 1898–99,	—	—	306,978 0 0
Carried forward,	—	—	323,465 17 10

of Public Works in the Year ended 31st March, 1898.

VOTES AND GRANTS.

EXPENDITURE.	£ s. d.	£ s. d.	£ s. d.	£ s. d.
Balances on Parliamentary Votes, 1897-98, surrendered to H.M. Exchequer, viz.:—				
Public Works and Buildings,		—	12,979 4 6	
Office of Public Works,		—	1,833 16 7	
Railways, Ireland,		—	38 4 8	13,[illegible] 6 8
Public Works and Buildings—Class I. Vote 13:—				
Purchase of Sites and Buildings. Sub-Head A.—				
Land Commission,		8,507 7 6		
Military Probate Office,		451 7 4		
Science and Art Museum (Leinster Lawn),		2,313 3 0		
Central Bridewell,		2,408 16 7		
Coastguard Stations,		284 17 7	6,964 13 10	
New Works and Alterations. Sub-Head B.:—				
Royal Hospital,		1,317 18 2		
Royal Hibernian Military School,		531 6 6		
Coastguard and Naval Reserve Buildings,		2,536 17 8		
Ordnance Survey Buildings,		28 2 6		
State Residences,		840 4 1		
Chief Secretary's Office,		6 19 10		
Stationery Office,		165 6 6		
Office of Public Works,		478 6 3		
General Register Office,		147 10 4		
High Court of Justice,		431 17 9		
Probate Offices,		162 0 0		
Registration of Titles Office,		257 10 7		
Land Commission Court and Offices,		898 4 0		
Metropolitan Police Buildings,		183 16 10		
Constabulary,		983 16 8		
Dundrum Criminal Lunatic Asylum,		1,148 17 11		
Science and Art Buildings, including Botanic Gardens,		1,553 11 1		
National Education Buildings:—				
Albert Model Farm,	478 5 3			
Munster Model Farm,	132 14 7			
National Schools,	37,161 16 3			
Model Schools,	837 18 6			
Teachers' Residences,	—	33,786 14 11		
Queen's Colleges,		359 13 9		
Customs and Inland Revenue,		2,483 4 8		
Postal and Telegraph Buildings,		10,548 7 7		
Phœnix Park,		85 0 6		
Kingstown Harbour,		905 8 0		
Temporary Commissioners—Congested Districts Board,		204 0 7	64,023 4 1	
Carried forward,		—	83,926 17 11	13,[illegible] 5 9

AN ACCOUNT showing the RECEIPTS and EXPENDITURE of the COMMISSIONERS

(G 1.)—PARLIAMENTARY

RECEIPTS—*continued.*

	£ s. d.	£ s. d.	£ s. d.
Brought forward, . .	—	—	321,165 17 10
I. PUBLIC WORKS AND BUILDINGS—*continued.*			
PARTICULARS OF RECEIPTS (APPROPRIATIONS IN AID). Shown on the other side:—			
Buildings:—The sums received were mostly for Rents, .	—	4,375 3 1	
Parks—Phoenix Park:—			
Rents, . . .	533 8 8		
Sales, &c., . . .	89 13 5		
		623 1 1	
St. Stephen's Green:—			
Sales, . . .	—	40 6 8	
Harbours—Kingstown:—			
Dues, ...	1,130 8 4		
Rents, ...	340 10 10		
Water supplied to Shipping, . . .	75 18 0		
Hire and Sale of Plant, . . .	10 19 9		
Sale of Old Materials, . . .	313 18 8		
Rent Limestone, . . .	3 7 6		
Yacht Slip—use of, and Storage of Yachts, .	69 0 0		
Sundries, ...	0 6 7		
		1,761 1 8	
Howth:—			
Dues, . .	56 15 6		
Rents, . .	266 8 0		
Sales, &c., .	1 3 0		
		334 6 6	
Donaghadee:—			
Dues, . .	—		
Rents, . .	11 14 0		
Sales, &c., .	—		
		11 14 0	
Ardglass:—			
Dues, . . .	83 4 10		
Rents, . . .	7 5 0		
Sales, &c., . .	—		
		90 19 10	
Dunmore:—			
Dues, . . .	34 11 4		
Rents, . . .	65 16 5		
Sales, &c., . .	—		
		80 7 9	
		7,326 17 8	
River Shannon Works (see page 55), . .	—	15 18 10	
		7,342 10 6	
Carried forward, . .	—	—	328,408 17 10

An Account showing the Receipts and Expenditure of the Commission[illegible]

(G 1.)—PARLIAMENTARY

RECEIPTS—continued.	£ s. d.	£ s. d.	£ s. d.
Brought forward, .	—	—	223,406 17 10
1. Public Buildings—continued.			
1. Drainage Works—River Shannon, . .	—	—	—
2. Railways, Ireland, Acts, 1883, 1889, and 1893:—			
(a), (b), and (c) Vote.—Class I. No. 14, . .	—	—	93,207 0 0
3. Light Railways (Ireland) Act, 1889 (Non-voting Account):—			
Received from National Debt Commissioners, . .	—	—	—
„ „ other sources, . . .	—	103 3 7	103 3 7
Carried forward, .	—	—	316,718 1 5

of Public Works in the Year ended 31st March, 1899.

VOTES AND GRANTS—continued.

EXPENDITURE—continued.	£ s. d.	£ s. d.	£ s. d.
Brought forward,	—	104,318 17 9	13,986 8 9
1. Public Buildings—continued.			
Drainage Works—River Shannon, Sub-Head H.,	304 9 10		
Less Appropriations in Aid,	25 18 10		
		278 11 0	
			126,067 8 9
2. Railways, Ireland:—			
Vote—Class I. No. 14.			
(a) Repayments to Baronies under Tramways and Public Companies Act, 1883.			
County. — Railway.			
Cavan, — Cavan and Leitrim,	—	606 17 8	
Clare, — South Clare,	—	2,223 7 3	
" — West Clare,	—	2,958 4 7	
Cork, — Cork and Muskerry,	—	1,759 13 8	
" — Donoughmore Extension,	—	900 0 0	
" — Mitchelstown and Fermoy,	—	1,764 6 7	
" — Schull and Skibbereen,	—	1,710 0 0	
" — Timoleague and Courtmacsherry,	—	1,030 0 0	
Donegal, — Donegal and Killybegs,	—	80 0 0	
" — Stranorlar and Glenties,	—	3 0 0	
" — West Donegal (Druminin to Donegal),	—	979 11 4	
Dublin, — Dublin and Blessington,	—	788 18 11	
Fermanagh, — Clogher Valley,	—	485 16 8	
Galway, — Loughrea and Attymon,	—	918 14 8	
Kerry, — Headford and Kenmare,	—	1,200 0 0	
" — Killorglin and Valentia,	—	1,400 0 0	
" — Tralee and Dingle,	—	1,150 0 0	
Leitrim, — Cavan and Leitrim,	—	2,083 6 8	
Mayo, — Claremorris and Swinford,	—	179 13 3	
" — Ballinrobe and Claremorris,	—	619 4 5	
" — Athenry and Tuam (Extension to Claremorris),	—	1,381 18 4	
Sligo, — Collooney and Swinford,	—	910 8 11	
Tyrone, — Clogher Valley,	—	3,926 8 5	
Wicklow, — Dublin and Blessington,	—	836 7 4	
Tralee Town, — Tralee and Dingle,	—	100 0 0	
		27,177 11 3	
(b) Instalments of Annuities in repayment of Advances by National Debt Commissioners (£537,008), under Railway Acts, 1889 and 1893,	—	64,199 16 0	
(c) Do. do. (£10,000) under Railways Act, 1896,	—	497 7 6	
			91,874 14 9
Light Railways (Ireland) Act, 1889 (Non-voted Account)			
Donegal and Killybegs Railway,	—	12 15 11	
Stranorlar and Glenties,	—	1,455 4 8	
			1,467 0 8
Carried forward,	—	—	213,349 9 10

1

An Account showing the Receipts and Expenditure of the Commissioners

(G 1.)—PARLIAMENTARY

RECEIPTS—continued.	£ s. d.	£ s. d.	£ s. d.
Brought forward,	—	—	314,716 1 0
4. Tramways (Ireland) Act, 1896 (Non-voted Amount):— Received from National Debt Commissioners,	—	—	*69,167 0 0
5. Railways Act, 1896 (Non-voted Amount):— Received from National Debt Commissioners,	—	30,000 0 0	
Received in respect of Traffic Receipts,	—	477 13 11	*30,477 13 11
6. Office of Public Works. Class II. Vote No. 8:— Vote,	—	—	65,119 6 9
Carried forward,	—	—	472,476 15 4

of Public Works in the Year ended 31st March, 1899.

VOTES AND GRANTS—continued.

EXPENDITURE—continued.	£ s. d.	£ s.
Brought forward,	—	—
4. Tramways (Ireland), Act, 1883. (Non-voted Account):—		
Amounts paid in redemption of Treasury contribution to Tramway Guarantees, 46 & 47 Vic., c. 43.		
West Donegal Light Railway,	—	9,187 0
Tralee and Dingle Light Railway,	—	50,000 0
5. Railways Act, 1896. (Non-voted Account):—		
Railways:—		
Buncrana and Carndonagh,	—	194 5
Letterkenny and Burtonport,	—	9,[illegible] 11
Steamer Services:—		
(a.) Killaloe and Dromod,	1,500 0 0	
(b.) Sligo and Belmullet (and Pier north of Belmullet, with Approach Road),	858 5 3	
(c.) New Piers on Lough Derg in connection with (a),	687 4 0	
		3,0[illegible] [illegible]
Coach and Steamer Services:—		
Listowel and Tarbert Coach,	879 19 6	
Tarbert and Kilrush Steamer,	1,178 17 4	
Ennistymon and Ballyvaughan Coach,	363 15 0	
Bantry and Dromod Coach,	285 7 8	
		2,6[illegible]7 16
General charges,	—	679 18

An Account showing the Receipts and Expenditure of the Commissioners

(G 1.)—Parliamentary

RECEIPTS—continued.	£ s. d.	£ s. d.	£ s. d.
Brought forward,	—	—	472,472 15 6
(F) Appropriations in aid of Votes for 1897–8.			
Public Buildings:—			
Inland Revenue Buildings—New Works,	902 19 4	902 19 4	
Royal Hospital, Maintenance,	17 18 9		
Dublin Castle, do.,	1 15 7		
Viceregal Lodge, do.,	8 10 11		
Office of Public Works, do.,	1 16 6		
High Court of Justice, do.,	17 1 6		
Royal Irish Constabulary Huts, do.,	2 16 6		
Science and Art Museum, do.,	4 7 6		
Queen's Colleges (Belfast), do.,	8 8 3		
Custom Buildings, do.,	5 4 4		
Inland Revenue Buildings, do.,	0 6 10		
Post Office do., do.,	1 4 6		
Telegraph do., do.,	0 5 9		
Congested Districts Board, do.,	0 12 11		
Kingstown Harbour, do.,	2,[illegible] 17 7	2,[illegible] 4 9	
Custom Buildings—Furniture,	1 5 0		
Telegraph do., do.,	18 12 11	19 18 11	
Land Commission—Rents,	16 17 2		
Geological Survey, do.,	4 0 6	20 17 8	
Chief Secretary's Office, Fuel,	7 7 1		
Police Courts and Offices, do.,	3 18 4		
Royal Irish Constabulary Depot, do.,	8 12 6		
General Prisons Office, do.,	3 13 7	23 [illegible] [illegible]	
Office of Public Works:—			
Salaries,	0 16 0		
Travelling Expenses,	2 10 0		
Land Improvement Loans,	0 1 6		
Appropriations in Aid,	0 10 0		

of Public Works, in the Year ended 31st March, 1899.

Votes and Grants—continued.

Expenditure—continued.	£ s. d.	£ s. d.
Brought forward,	—	—
4. Adjustments affecting the Votes for 1897-8.		
Public Buildings:—		
Land Commission—Purchase of Sites,	—	13 17 3
Kingstown Harbour, New Works,	—	245 17 0
Customs Buildings, Maintenance,	1 5 0	
Inland Revenue Buildings, do.,	[illegible] 10 4	803 17 [illegible]
Dublin Castle State Apartments, Furniture,	1 3 10	
Vice-Regal Lodge, do.,	2 17 4	
Office of Public Works, do.,	1 13 6	
High Court of Justice, do.,	13 1 6	
Science and Art Museum, do.,	5 7 6	
Queen's College, Belfast, do.,	2 2 5	
Customs Buildings, do.,	5 5 5	
Inland Revenue Buildings, do.,	0 6 10	
Post Office do., do.,	1 4 8	
Telegraph do., do.,	0 1 2	
Congested Districts Board, do.,	0 10 11	33 15 2
Inland Revenue Buildings, Rents,	—	1 9 11
Kingstown Harbour, Fuel,	—	1 8 0
Kingstown Harbour, Compensation,	—	1,924 14 7
River Shannon Works,	—	90 0 0
Office of Public Works:—		
Travelling Expenses,	3 0 0	
Incidental,	0 15 0	
Land Improvement Loans,	1 1 11	4 16 11
Balance—Cash,	—	54,529 6 1
Imprests,	—	4,331 0 0
Grants undrawn from the Exchequer,	—	1,017 4 8

(G 2.)—An Account showing the Receipts and Expenditure of the Commissioners

PUBLIC WORKS LOANS

	£ s. d.	£ s. d.
To Balance, 1st April, 1898,	—	33,3[illegible] 11 [illegible]
" Public Works Loans:		
Vote of Credit 1897–98, £1,000,000—National Debt Commissioners,	200,000 0 0	
" 1898–99, £800,000— "	440,000 0 0	
		640,000 0 0

of Public Works in the Year ended 31st March, 1899.

ADVANCES.

	£ s. d.			£ s. d.
By Public Works Loans,				
Amount advanced on Loans, viz.:—				
Grand Juries of Counties,	3,430	1	10	
Local Boards,	1,600	0	0	
Quarries, Mines, and Miscellaneous,	10,000	0	0	
Harbours, Docks, &c.,	3,142	6	6	
Housing of the Working Classes,	30,518	0	0	
Glebe Loans, 33 & 34 Vic., c. 112,	14,368	0	0	
Public Health, 37 & 38 Vic., c. 93,	74,918	19	7	
River Drainage, 36 & 37 Vic., c. 33,	2,250	0	0	
Post Roads, for Repairs, 6 & 7 Wm. IV., c. 116,	160	11	1	
Land Improvement Preliminary Expenses,	3,200	0	0	
Repairs of Fishery Piers,	500	0	0	
Seed Supply, 1890,	66,387	15	4	
Lunatic Asylums Buildings, 1 & 2 Geo. IV., c. 33,	344,585	10	11	
Labourers' Acts,	110,016	0	0	
Land Improvement, 10 Vic., c. 32, &c.,	30,477	0	0	
National School Teachers' Residences,	7,349	0	0	
Dispensary Houses,	6,130	0	0	
Workhouse Buildings, &c.,	3,600	0	0	
Non-Vested Schools and Training Colleges,	5,380	0	0	
Land Law, 44 & 45 Vic., c. 49, s. 31,	18,943	0	0	
				841,195 5 3

(G 3.)—An Account showing the Receipts and Expenditure of the Commissioners

PUBLIC WORKS LOANS

	Repayments (Principal and Interest).			Totals.		
To Public Works Loans:—	£	s.	d.	£	s.	d.
Amounts received in repayment:—						
Grand Juries of Counties,	7,868	1	3			
Local Boards,	6,635	3	5			
Roads and Bridges,	10,165	16	6			
Inland Navigations,	736	9	3			
Public Buildings,	2,330	3	0			
Railways,	22,031	9	6			
Quarries, Mines, and Miscellaneous,	271	15	8			
Harbours, Docks, &c.,	14,628	6	1			
Labourers' Dwellings in Towns,	10,977	17	6			
Artisans' Dwellings,	910	11	9			
Housing of the Working Classes,	16,633	9	8			
Glebe Loans,	28,750	12	8			
Public Health,	92,868	5	4			
River Drainage Maintenance, 29 & 30 Vic., c. 49, &c.,	1,233	16	7			
River Drainage, 26 & 27 Vic., c. 88,	34,736	9	6			
Loans per Act 57 Geo. III., c. 34,	160	0	0			
Post Roads, Repairs,	215	7	0			
Land Improvement Preliminary Expenses,	2,083	5	9			
Lunatic Asylums Buildings,	50,129	19	8			
Building Schools,	24	14	0			
Seed Supply, 1880,	630	4	11			
" 1890,	25	7	6			
" 1895,	176	11	3			
" 1898,	6,739	0	5			
Emigration,	501	8	4			
Labourers' Acts,	84,150	1	2			
Land Improvement Loans,	99,501	18	6			
National School Teachers' Residences,	8,180	15	0			
Dispensary Houses,	5,146	17	7			
Non-Vested Schools and Training Colleges,	2,990	2	8			
Land Law, 44 & 45 Vic., c. 49, s. 31,	65,184	19	7			
Land Act Loans, 33 & 34 Vic., c. 46,	13,845	10	6			
				606,194	9	3
Local Loans Fund Premium Account,	—			16	17	7
To Church Fund Loans:—						
Land Improvement,	33,886	3	7			
Sanitary,	1,407	13	6			
Baronial Works,	4,316	17	3			
Arterial Drainage,	77	4	7			
				39,549	17	10
				646,761	4	8

Office of Public Works, Dublin, 20th June, 1899.

(G 4.)—LAND IMPROVEMENT

RECEIPTS.	£	s.	d.	£	s.	d.
Amount received from National Debt Commissioners by way of Loan,	1,200	0	0			
" " from Proprietors in Repayment of Preliminary Expenses,	1,109	9	8			
				2,309	9	8
				2,309	9	8

of Public Works, in the Year ended 31st March, 1899.

REPAYMENTS.

	£ s. d.	£ s. d.
By amounts transferred to National Debt Commissioners,	—	608,914 9 3
Ditto,	—	16 17 7
By amount transferred to Irish Land Commissioners,	—	39,849 17 10
		648,781 4 8

G. H. [illegible], Accountant.

(G 5.)—LUNATIC

AN ACCOUNT showing the RECEIPTS and EXPENDITURE by the COMMISSIONERS of PUBLIC WORKS, IRELAND, (on 1899, pursuant to Act 1 & 2

RECEIPTS.	£ s. d.	£ s. d.	£ s. d.
Balance from last Account,	—	—	31,543 6 7
Amounts received from the Local Loan Fund on account of Loans to the following District Asylums, and other receipts:—			
Antrim,	—	21,804 3 3	
Armagh,	—	6,187 9 6	
Ballinasloe,	—	15,580 3 9	
Belfast,	—	3,700 0 0	
Carlow,	—	7,186 8 7	
Castlebar,	—	1,310 0 0	
Clonmel,	—	1,838 16 11	
Cork,	—	14,481 2 5	
Downpatrick,	—	10,200 0 0	
Ennis,	—	397 11 5	
Enniscorthy,	—	10,500 0 0	
Kilkenny,	—	5,850 0 0	
Killarney,	—	1,101 16 7	
Letterkenny,	—	4,085 8 1	
Limerick,	—	5,802 11 0	
Londonderry,	—	3,957 17 9	
Maryborough,	—	9,672 10 1	
Monaghan,	—	4,793 12 1	
Mullingar,	—	6,113 1 0	
Omagh,	—	16,269 16 5	
Richmond,	—	33,760 10 10	
Sligo,	—	5,037 0 0	
Waterford,	—	9,150 0 9	
			217,828 13 4
			249,371 19 11

Office of Public Works, Dublin, 17th May, 1899.

(G 6.)—SEA FISHERIES

AN ACCOUNT showing the RECEIPTS and EXPENDITURE by the COMMISSIONERS of PUBLIC WORKS

RECEIPTS.	£ s. d.	£ s. d.
Balance from last Account,	—	18,387 5 8
Amounts received in repayment of Loan—		
Ballydavid Pier,	63 1 4	
Liscannor Harbour,	140 15 0	
Kilkee Boat Slip,	24 9 0	
Annalong Harbour,	78 15 6	
Kilkeel Harbour,	188 19 8	
Culdaff Pier,	36 8 9	
Port Salon Pier,	133 18 0	
Portstewart Harbour,	149 0 0	
Malin Head Pier,	334 18 8	
Cleggan Pier,	319 11 10	
Carlingford Harbour,	858 12 10	
Carrigaholt Harbour,	298 11 4	
Kilmore Harbour,	214 6 3	
Ballywalter Pier,	139 18 6	
Clogher Head Breakwater,	538 17 10	
Seafield Pier,	108 6 0	
Greystones Pier,	137 7 0	

ASYLUMS BUILDINGS.

Account of the Commissioners for the Control, &c., of Lunatic Asylums) during the year ended 31st March, Geo. IV., c. 33, &c., &c.

EXPENDITURE.	£ s. d.	£ s. d.	£ s. d.
Amounts expended on the following District Asylums, viz.:—			
Antrim,	—	29,653 7 2	
Armagh,	—	3,544 8 0	
Ballinasloe,	—	10,334 7 3	
Belfast,	—	5,273 9 4	
Carlow,	—	7,171 18 4	
Castlebar,	—	1,601 10 –	
Clonmel,	—	2,036 11 8	
Cork,	—	16,140 1 5	
Downpatrick,	—	11,170 18 5	
Ennis,	—	279 12 7	
Enniscorthy,	—	10,364 12 1	
Kilkenny,	—	4,730 2 11	
Killarney,	—	1,047 1 1	
Letterkenny,	—	1,229 4 6	
Limerick,	—	3,708 5 9	
Londonderry,	—	4,113 16 1	
Maryborough,	—	9,081 3 8	
Monaghan,	—	4,770 0 3	
Mullingar,	—	8,017 1 10	
Omagh,	—	14,281 4 2	
Richmond	—	73,183 1 5	
Sligo,	—	5,510 8 11	
Waterford,	—	9,218 11 3	
			256,708 7 8
Balance—Cash,	—	—	12,863 11 3
			269,571 18 11

G. H. Saldwell, Accountant.

(IRELAND) COMMISSION.

Ireland, during the Year ended 31st March, 1899, pursuant to Act 46 & 47 Victoria, cap. 26.

EXPENDITURE.	£ s. d.	£ s. d.
Expenses of Engineering Staff,	360 3 4	360 3 4

(G 7.)—An Account showing the Receipts and Expenditure by the Commissioners

MISCELLANEOUS

RECEIPTS.	£ s. d.	£ s. d.	£ s. d.
To Balance from last Account,	—	—	[illegible] 7 1
1. Deposits for Preliminary Expenses on Loans, &c.:— Received from Sundries,	—	—	1,041 6 10
2. Railway and other Arbitration Expenses, 14 & 15 Vic., c. 70:— Received from Railway Companies and others, to meet Expenses of Arbitrations,	—	—	[illegible]
3. Arterial Drainage Deposits, 26 & 27 Vic., c. 88, &c.:— Received from Drainage Boards on Account of Preliminary and other Expenses,	—	—	2 2 0
4. Piers—Works—9 Vic., c. 3:—			
5. Piers—Repairs—16 & 17 Vic., c. 136:— Ardmore Pier, county Galway,	—	—	[illegible]
6. Inland Navigation:— Shannon River:—			
Rents,	—	2,719 10 3	
Tolls,	[illegible] 19 11	—	
Less rebate allowed to Grand Canal Company,	60 16 1	—	
		2,815 3 7	
Sale of old Steamer, &c.,	—	70 8 0	
Contribution to meet cost of repairs to Crane,	—	14 10 0	
			5,645 0 10

of Public Works, Ireland, during the Year ended 31st March, 1899.

SERVICES.

EXPENDITURE.	£ s. d.	£ s. d.	£ s. d.
1. Deposits for Preliminary Expenses of Loans, &c.:— Paid to Sundries, ...	—	—	817 19 8
2. Railway and other Arbitration Expenses, 14 & 15 Vic., c. 70:— Paid to Valuators, &c., ...	—	—	3,780 16 1
3. Arterial Drainage Deposits, 26 & 27 Vic., c. 88, &c.:— Paid on account of Fees, &c., ...	—	—	67 10 7
4. Piers—Works—9 Vic., c. 3:—			
5. Piers—Repairs—16 & 17 Vic., c. 136:— Ardwan Pier, Co. Galway, . . .	—	—	833 14 11

(G 7.)—An Account showing the Receipts and Expenditure of the Commissioners

MISCELLANEOUS

RECEIPTS—continued.	£ s. d.	£ s. d.	£ s. d.
Brought forward,	—	—	16,8[illegible]5 3 [illegible]
7. National Monuments, 32 & 33 Vic., c. 42, and 44 & 45 Vic., c. 46:—			
Sale of Stock,	—	—	
Dividends on Stock,	—	910 19 0	
Refund of Income Tax, &c.,	—	123 10 3	
			1,034 [illegible] [illegible]
8. Sea and Coast Fisheries Fund, 47 & 48 Vic., c. 21, and 54 & 55 Vic., c. 48:—Non-congested Districts—			
Dividends,	—	365 0 0	
Sale of Stock,	—	Nil	
Repayments of Loans,	—	3,061 3 1	
			[illegible] 3 1
9. Linen Hall, 41 Vic., c. 1:—			
Rents,	—	—	464 [illegible] [illegible]
10. Galway Harbour Receiver's Account:—			
Dues, &c.,	—	—	3,284 6 5
Carried forward,	—	—	25,439 3 10

of Public Works in the Year ended 31st March, 1879.

SERVICES—continued.

EXPENDITURE—continued.	£ s. d.	£ s. d.	£ s. d.
Brought forward,	—	—	10,847 2 2
7. National Monuments, 32 & 33 Vic., c. 42, and 55 & 56 Vic., c. 46:—			
Maintenance—			
Salaries and Travelling Expenses of Architect; Caretakers' Wages, Incidents, &c.,	—	422 8 4	
Works—			
St. Columb's House, Kells,	11 12 0		
Bective Abbey,	6 6 1		
Clare Abbey,	60 6 5		
Donegal Abbey,	43 4 5		
Kells Abbey,	63 14 0		
		184 17 2	
			607 5 6
8. Sea and Coast Fisheries Fund, 37 & 38 Vic., c. 31, and 51 & 55 Vic., c. 45:—Non-congested Districts—			
Advances on Loans,	—	—	2,043 7 10
9. Linen Hall, 41 Vic., c. 1:—			
Rent, &c.,	—	150 0 0	
Pension (1½ years) of late Secretary,	—	25 0 0	
Transfer to Her Majesty's Exchequer,	—	300 0 0	
			475 0 0
10. Galway Harbour Receiver's Account:—			
Repayment of Loan,	—	2,470 18 0	
Salaries, Maintenance of Works, &c.,	—	1,093 8 7	
			3,563 ? 7
Carried forward,	—	—	17,054 18 8

(G 7.)—An Account showing the Receipts and Expenditure of the Commissioners

MISCELLANEOUS

RECEIPTS—continued.	£ s. d.	£ s. d.	£ s. d.
Brought forward,	—	—	[illegible],430 3 10
11. [illegible] Railway:—			
Revenue, after deduction of Working Company's charge, for year ended 31st December, 1898,	—	4,161 18 4	
Amount received for payment of Baronial Guaranteed Dividends,	—	3,145 0 0	
			7,3[illegible] 18 4
12. Letterkenny Railway:—			
Balance of Revenue after deduction of Working Company's charge, for half year ended 31st December, 1897,	—	326 9 0	
Revenue (after deduction of Working Company's charge), for year ended 31st December, 1898,	—	3,115 14 0	
			3,441 3 0
13. Sundry Accounts:—			
Curragh of Kildare—Rents,	—	80 1 1	
Land Commission (Church Property Department),	—	910 0 0	
Four Courts, Law Library,	—	—	
Royal Dublin Society—Lecture Theatre,	—	138 18 9	
Chief Secretary's Gardens,	—	647 7 11	
Board of Admiralty,	—	35 13 8	
Board of Trade,	—	230 15 8	
Island Bridge Waterworks,	—	19 8 3	
Mountgarrett Bridge,	—	201 16 1	
Loans Insurance,	—	917 14 3	
Income Tax,	—	943 3 4	
Fishery Loan Fund—Surveys,	—	3 14 3	
Contractors' Deposits lodged with Tenders,	—	75 1 0	
Drainage Works—Closing Accounts,	—	13 9 0	
Dividends on Stock lodged as Contractors' Security,	—	5 16 1	
Labourers' Dwellings Loans, Receivers' Accounts,	—	233 8 6	
Railway (Ireland) Act, 1896—Traffic Receipts,	—	391 13 3	
Temporary Charges—for lodgment to Votes, Loans, &c.,	—	1,373 16 6	
			6,0[illegible] 7 1

of Public Works in the year ended 31st March, 1899.

SERVICES—continued.

EXPENDITURE—continued.	£ s. d.	£	s.
Brought forward,	—	—	
11. [illegible] Railway:—			
Interest on Loan,	—	3,600	0
Gt. S. & W. Railway Co.—Rent of Tuam Station,	—	929	6
General Charges,	—	557	11
Dividends on Baronial Guaranteed Stock (year to 31st December, 1898),	—	2,146	0
12. Letterkenny Railway:—			
Interest on Loan,	—	3,330	0
General Charges,	—	148	1
13. Sundry Accounts:—			
Curragh of Kildare—Payment to Commissioners of Woods and Forests,	—	87	8
Land Commission (Church Property Department),	—	257	4
Four Courts, Law Library,	—	131	0
Royal Dublin Society—Lecture Theatre,	—	156	8
Chief Secretary's Gardens,	—	494	15
Board of Admiralty—Costs of preparing Leases,	—	10	17
Board of Trade—Building Rocket Cart Houses, &c.,	—	390	8
Island Bridge Waterworks,	—	14	15
Mountgarrett Bridge,	—	7	3
Lease Insurance,	—	208	15
Income Tax,	—	600	2
Fishery Loan Funds—Stamps,	—	3	18
Contractors' Deposits refunded,	—	65	0
Drainage Works—Closing Account,	—	1	10
Dividends on Stock lodged as Contractor's Security,	—	3	18
Labourers' Dwellings Loans, Receivers' Accounts,	—	320	10
Railways (Ireland) Act, 1896—Transfer to votes,	—	678	0
Payments in respect of Temporary Receipts,	—	3,075	8

(G 2.)—Arterial

These Works are executed by [illegible]

Schedule.—Abstract of Final Awards

Districts.	Counties.	Date when Awards made final.	Area of Flooded or Injured Lands, which have been Drained or Improved Under the Schemes.			Cost per Acre to Proprietors, of the Drainage, including Interest, &c.			Increase in the Annual Letting Value of those Lands, caused by Drainage.		
			A.	R.	P.	£	s.	d.	£	s.	d.
Athboy River,	Meath,	4th April, 1859,	1,[illegible]	0	27	6	0	4	380	10	8
Ballinamuddy,	Limerick,	2nd Oct., 1875,	179	0	6	7	1	2	82	4	1
Ballyadams,	Queen's,	9th Oct., 1863,	[illegible]	2	0	4	6	9	194	16	0
Ballymilton,	Tipperary,	8th Oct., 1861,	297	1	18	4	14	8	93	7	8
Ballymacurrig,	King's and Queen's,	9th April, 1868,	2,[illegible]	1	22	9	7	4	316	14	0
Ballyteigue & Kilmore,	Wexford,	9th Oct., 1866,	6,970	3	27	6	9	10	1,325	4	2
Baltracey,	Kildare,	10th Mar., 1876,	1,[illegible]	0	06	4	0	4	[illegible]	4	0
Barnakyle,	Limerick,	2nd April, 1867,	1,017	1	32	9	16	1	697	10	9
Bealacorrig,	King's,	27th Mar., 1878,	[illegible]	0	76	3	7	1	197	17	0
Brickey River,	Waterford,	28th Sept., 1870,	[illegible]	1	20	6	6	5	997	2	1
Bride River,	Cork,	9th Oct., 1862,	1,297	0	1	0	18	6	821	3	8
Bunkay,	Limerick,	8 Oct., 1864,	[illegible]	1	20	1	10	2	120	2	4
Camoge,	Limerick,	26th Sept., 1876,	1,2[illegible]	3	0	2	8	1	677	4	6
Carrigrohane, &c.,	Cork,	Not yet under Award.									
Clodiagh River,	Tipperary,	30th May, 1878,	1,487	1	4	1	3	7	[illegible]	0	7
Cashen,	Kerry,	9th Oct., 1867,	4,794	2	19	2	2	0	[illegible]	16	4
[illegible]	Kildare,	16th Jan., 1870,	747	2	9	3	0	4	171	18	8
Corrygrane,	Longford,	9th Oct., 1862,	116	0	27	5	2	4	37	16	1
Derrinlough,	King's,	8th Oct., 1874,	672	0	20	5	4	3	143	18	4
Doohyle,	Limerick,	9th Oct., 1871,	469	0	02	4	8	7	145	9	8
Douglas River,	Carlow,	31st Mar., 1874,	4,0[illegible]	2	0	4	7	8	929	19	0
Elphin,	Roscommon,	28th Mar., 1872,	5,916	3	12	4	11	3	1,026	1	10
Folliamount,	Meath,	8th Oct., 1860,	201	0	22	5	3	1	49	8	8
Do.,	Do.,	9th Oct., 1861,	—			—			—		
Frankford River,	King's,	27th Mar., 1876,	1,394	3	0	5	4	3	414	16	8
Do.,	Do.,	4th April, 1884,	—			—			—		
Garristown and Delvin,	Meath and Dublin,	3rd April, 1876,	5,253	0	12	1	5	4	481	0	0
Glashaboy,	Cork,	4th April, 1866,	133	1	0	10	5	4	111	14	8

RS, &c.

Provisions of the above Acts.

ar ended 31st March, 1890.

Portion of [illegible] Advance charged to [illegible] Public Works, [illegible] by [illegible] Board.			Amount charged on Lands.			Receipts (Principal and Interest).									District.
						To [illegible] March, 18[illegible].			For year ended 31st March, 18[illegible].			Total to 31st March, 18[illegible].			
£	s.	d.	£	s.	d.	£	s.	d.	£	s.	d.	£	s.	d.	
–			11,141	18	2	13,353	1[illegible]	3	–			13,0[illegible]	14	6	[illegible] River.
–			1,[illegible]	8	10	1,[illegible]	[illegible]	7	87	10	6	1,7[illegible]	1[illegible]	1	[illegible]
[illegible]	10	0	3,[illegible]	1[illegible]	6	3,44[illegible]	1[illegible]	8	[illegible]	1	6	3,[illegible]	13	5	Ballyn[illegible].
67 [illegible] *[illegible]	10 [illegible]	0 6	1,[illegible]	18	6	7[illegible]	16	4	[illegible]	3	10	[illegible]	2	4	Bally[illegible].
–			[illegible]	[illegible]	1	[illegible]	1[illegible]	1	–			6,4[illegible]	10	1	Bally[illegible].
–			15,741	6	[illegible]	[illegible]	13	5	[illegible]	10	11	[illegible]	16	4	Bally[illegible] and

(G 5.)—ARTERIAL DRAINAGE,—

These Works are executed by District Boards in [illegible]

SCHEDULE.—ABSTRACT of FINAL AWARDS, and Receipts [illegible]

[illegible]	[illegible]	Date when Awards made final.	Area of Flooded or Injured Lands, which have been Drained or Improved [illegible]	Cost per Acre to Proprietors of the Drainage, including [illegible]	Increase in the Annual Letting Value of those Lands, caused by Drainage.	Amount of Instalments payable [illegible]	[illegible]
			a. r. p.	£ s. d.	£ s. d.	£ s. d.	
	Brought forward,	. . . .	55,236 0 3	—	20,155 7 8	2,140 8 0	
Grenagh, . . .	Limerick, . . .	6th April, 1868, .	2,259 0 24	5 0 4	546 0 0	267 11 4	65
Gully, ...	Queen's, . . .	4th Oct., 1873, .	1,064 0 16	4 4 11	847 10 8	[illegible]	[illegible]
Gully Upper, . .	Queen's, . . .	14th Mar., 1876,	509 1 15	4 15 3	170 12 0	35 4 8	45
Hogan's Pass, . .	Tipperary, . . .	5th Oct., 1868, .	845 1 23	5 15 0	280 15 10	101 1 0	65
Inny, Upper, . .	Meath, Westmeath, Longford, & Cavan,	4th April, 1861,	11,078 2 7	7 0 0	2,780 2 4	1,648 1 5	25
Island Lake and Glore River,	Mayo, . . .	2nd April, 1878,	1,467 0 33	5 10 0	462 5 6	146 16 10	67
Kildare, . . .	Kildare, . . .	23rd Sept., 1877,	4,557 3 30	1 11 6	486 7 10	33 1 11	[illegible]
Killard, . . .	Cork, . . .	9th Oct., 1854, .	201 1 0	1 4 1	163 16 3	48 6 0	45
Kilmastulla, . .	Tipperary, . . .	28th July, 1878,	1,441 1 16	6 10 7	385 18 8	—	[illegible]
Lorum, . . .	Meath, . . .	3rd April, 1868,	470 1 22	7 0 7	204 19 10	110 11 0	45
Lerr River, . .	Kildare and Carlow,	9th Oct., 1865, .	1,481 0 27	16 8 11	436 5 0	534 5 7	40
Lough Erne, . .	Cavan, Donegal, Fermanagh, & Monaghan,	4th April, 1861,	16,237 0 36	11 16 11	4,716 11 0	8,220 0 7	22
Do. (Navigation),	Do. . . .	—	—	—	—	354 8 4	22
Lough Oughter, . .	Cavan, . . .	4th April, 1879,	3,077 1 30	3 1 11	448 14 8	874 1 4	46
Millard, . . .	Cork, . . .	4th Oct., 1867, .	1,015 0 10	4 14 0	440 8 3	380 12 6	45
Morning Star, Upper,	Limerick, . . .	4th April, 1868,	630 0 23	1 12 0	535 1 0	173 10 6	48
Mulkear River, .	Limerick, . . .	22nd Sept., 1877,	3,300 0 24	1 4 1	823 0 11	441 16 3	41
Nanny River, . .	Meath, . . .	4th April, 1858,	784 1 4	10 0 1	386 14 0	187 19 5	40
Do. Upper, .	Do. . . .	4th April, 1866,	188 3 30	8 7 9	73 11 7	36 1 10	40
Owenure, . . .	Do. . . .	4th April, 1866,	4,287 0 0	5 9 5	801 7 6	779 0 11	40
Parsonstown, . .	Tipperary and King's,	25th Sept., 1876,	2,710 0 1	4 4 0	440 13 6	380 10 6	22
Quinagh, . . .	Carlow, . . .	19th Jan., 1876, .	480 5 0	2 13 4	200 1 5	—	[illegible]
Rathangan River, .	Kildare, . . .	4th April, 1862,	6,904 0 3	0 13 5	2,044 16 10	1,720 7 10	45
Rathdowney, . .	Queen's, . . .	9th Oct., 1868, .	415 1 20	4 0 1	169 0 4	—	[illegible]

26 & 27 Vic., c. 88, &c.

[illegible] with the Provisions of the above Acts.

[illegible], for the Year ended 31st March, 1899.

Total Amount Advanced, including Interest to date of Award.	Portion of Total Advances charged to Counties for Public Works, or refunded by Drainage Board.	Amount charged on Lands.	Receipts: Principal and Interest. To 31st March, 1898.	For year ended 31st March, 1899.	Total to 31st March, 1899.	Districts.
£ s. d.	£ s. d.	£ s. d.	£ s. d.	£ s. d.	£ s. d.	
168,727 1 8 / 2,310 0 0	2,077 16 3	[illegible] 11 5	[illegible] 16 0	4,[illegible] 1 3	[illegible] 19 3	
13,[illegible] 7 0	873 0 0 / *873 18 6	12,302 18 6	[illegible]	338 12 1	[illegible]	Gransagh.
4,217 11 8	–	4,217 11 8	[illegible]	[illegible]	[illegible]	Gully.
2,447 16 [illegible]	70 [illegible]	2,377 16 [illegible]	[illegible]	[illegible]	[illegible]	Gully, Upper.
[illegible] 18 0	[illegible]	[illegible]	3,[illegible]	[illegible]	[illegible] 16 [illegible]	Hogan's Pass.
[illegible]	2,107 13 [illegible] / *2,700 0 0	[illegible] 10 0	[illegible]	[illegible] 17 [illegible]	14,[illegible] 16 7	Lary, Upper.
[illegible] 11 7	715 0 0 / *100 0 0	[illegible] 10 7	[illegible] 16 [illegible]	418 16 1	[illegible] 7 [illegible]	Inland Lakes and Glen River.
[illegible]	[illegible] 0 0	[illegible]	10,[illegible] 11 [illegible]	[illegible]	10,[illegible] 19 1	Kildare.
1,[illegible]	–	1,[illegible]	[illegible]	[illegible]	311 16 4	Killord.
10,[illegible] 7 6	–	10,[illegible] 7 6	13,[illegible] 10 11	[illegible]	13,[illegible] 11	Kilmacrenan.
[illegible] 19 10	[illegible] 18 4	6,101 17 6	4,[illegible] 0 11	[illegible] 4 11	[illegible] 14 10	Laraner.
27,[illegible] 0 0	[illegible] 0 0	27,734 [illegible]	10,[illegible] 11 11	1,[illegible]	16,[illegible] 1	Lee River.
161,[illegible] 16 0	–	161,[illegible] 16 0	[illegible]	[illegible] 16 [illegible]	[illegible]	Lough Erne.
17,107 16 0	17,107 16 0	Nil.	18,[illegible]	1,104 [illegible]	19,[illegible] 14 0	Do., Navigation.
16,[illegible] 1 0	–	16,[illegible] 4 0	13,[illegible] 18 [illegible]	[illegible] 11 11	16,[illegible]	Lough Oughter.
[illegible] 14 6	–	[illegible] 14 6	[illegible] 18 0	[illegible]	[illegible]	Milford.
7,[illegible] 0 0	[illegible] 0 0	7,[illegible] 0 0	[illegible] 16 [illegible]	[illegible] 11	[illegible] 10 [illegible]	Morning Star, Upper.
30,774 0 0	[illegible] 1 0	[illegible] 10 0	[illegible] 10 11	1,[illegible] 7 [illegible]	[illegible] 19 3	Mulkear River.
[illegible] 5 1	[illegible] 0 0 / *[illegible] 19 7	[illegible]	[illegible] 10 0	[illegible]	[illegible] 16 0	Nanny River.
1,[illegible] 19 0	–	1,[illegible] 19 0	[illegible] 14 10	47 4 1	[illegible] 10 [illegible]	Do. Upper.
11,[illegible] 10 6	[illegible] 18 [illegible]	11,[illegible] 18 0	3,[illegible] 17 [illegible]	[illegible] 11	[illegible] 7 0	Owenreagh.
11,[illegible] 17 1	160 0 0	11,[illegible] 17 1	10,[illegible] 16 0	[illegible] 18 [illegible]	10,[illegible] 16 [illegible]	Pettigoe town.
[illegible] 10 6	*[illegible] 0 0	2,[illegible] 16 [illegible]	[illegible] 11 1	–	[illegible] 11 1	Quinagh.
77,[illegible] 6 [illegible]	1,[illegible] 0 0	76,[illegible] 6 9	[illegible]	[illegible]	[illegible] 5 1	Rathangan River.
[illegible] 6 6	–	2,[illegible]	2,[illegible] 6 7	–	[illegible] 6 7	Rathdowney.
[illegible]	–	[illegible]	[illegible]		[illegible]	Silver River.
[illegible] 13 11	[illegible] 1 [illegible]	[illegible] 19 3	[illegible]	[illegible] 0 0	[illegible] 7	Shannonbridge.
[illegible] 0 0	1,[illegible] 11 10 / *[illegible] 0 0	[illegible]	[illegible] 10 1	1,[illegible] 16 [illegible]	[illegible] 0 6	Scarryford River.
1[illegible] 0 [illegible]	1,[illegible] 6 6	137,633 [illegible] 11	[illegible]	[illegible] 5	[illegible] 16 [illegible]	Suck River.
13,[illegible] 0 0	13,[illegible] 0 0	–	[illegible] 0 0	741 5 0	[illegible] 16 0	Do.
[illegible] 5 6	163 0 0	1,[illegible] 5 6	[illegible] 18 [illegible]	[illegible] 0 [illegible]	[illegible] 15 0	Summerhill.
[illegible] 13 6	[illegible] 18 0 / *16 0 0	[illegible] 14 0	7,[illegible] 0	[illegible] 16 11	7,[illegible] 11	Swilly Burn.

(G 8.)—Arterial Drainage.—

These Works are executed by District Boards in

Schedule.—Abstract of Final Awards, and Receipts

Districts.	Counties.	Date when Awards made final.	Area of Flooded or Injured Lands, which have been Drained or Improved, Statute Measure.	Cost per Acre to Proprietors of the Drainage, including Interest, etc.	Increase in the Annual Letting Value of those Lands, caused by Drainage.	Amount of Instalments payable half-yearly, to repay Cost, with Interest, after deducting Redemptions.	[illegible]
			A. R. P.	£ s. d.	£ s. d.	£ s. d.	
	Brought forward,	—	222,897 0 16	—	26,[illegible] 5 6	16,377 [illegible] 1	—
Torrent River,	Tyrone,	2nd April, 1874,	488 1 16	11 [illegible] [illegible]	290 13 10	[illegible] / 88 11 7	[illegible]
Tory Hill,	Limerick,	2nd April, 1875,	901 3 2	6 6 6	454 10 4	140 9 0	10
[illegible],	Cork,	7th Sept., 1880,	[illegible] [illegible] 17	[illegible]	243 [illegible] 6	37 14 4 / 89 17 10	27 / 6
Ward River,	Dublin and Meath,	4th April, 1881,	[illegible] 0 18	7 16 [illegible]	514 7 8	182 19 6	[illegible]
	Total charge against districts,		[illegible] 1 30	Average 7 1 6	27,[illegible] 0 5	16,813 3 7	

Office of Public Works, Dublin, 30th June, 18[illegible].

56 & 57 Vic., c. 55, &c.

accordance with the Provisions of the above Acts.

thereon for the year ended 31st March, 1899.

[illegible]	[illegible]	Amount charged on Lands.	Receipts (Principal and Interest).			
			[illegible]	[illegible]	[illegible]	

APPENDIX H.

STATEMENT showing the PURPOSES for which ADVANCES of PUBLIC MONEY are made by the COMMISSIONERS of PUBLIC WORKS in IRELAND, with the RATES of INTEREST and PERIODS of REPAYMENT.

Purpose of Loan.	Authorising Acts.	Rate of Interest per cent. before Treasury Minute of [illegible] August, 1897.	Rate of Interest per cent. under Treasury Minute of [illegible] August, 1897.	Maximum Period of Repayment.
LOCAL LOANS FUND.				
Loans secured on Local Rates.				
1. County roads, bridges, and court-houses.	1 & 2 Wm. 4, c. 33, s. 22, amended by 31 & 32 Vict., c. 74, s. 1.	5		20 years.
2. Court-houses erected by the Board.	6 & 7 Wm. 4, c. 116, s. 70.	4		1 year from completion of works.
3. Bridges between counties, .	1 & 2 Wm. 4, c. 33, extended by 4 & 5 Wm. 4, c. 61, 2 & 3 Vict., c. 50, and 30 & 31 Vict., c. 50.	5		22 years.
4. Public works generally, including commercial harbours, docks, canals, and bridges other than county bridges.	1 & 2 Wm. 4, c. 33, with local or special Acts.	Not less than 4		25 years.
5. Fishery piers and harbours, construction of.	9 Vict. c. 3, and 29 and 30 Vict., c. 45.	5	3½	25 years.
6. Loans to Trustees of Districts carried out under the Act 5 & 6 Vict., c. 89.	43 & 44 Vict., c. 14, s. 13.	3½		15 years.
7. Repairs of post roads and bridges.	6 & 7 Wm. 4, c. 116, .	4		7 years.
8. Repairs of fishery piers, .	16 & 17 Vict., c. 136, sec. 11.	4		1 year from completion of works.
9. Maintenance of navigation works.	19 & 20 Vict., c. 62, .	4		Ditto.
10. Emigration, . . .	45 & 46 Vict., c. 67, .	3½ 3¾		20 years. 30 „
11. Public Buildings—				
(a) Public Libraries, . .	40 & 41 Vict., c. 15 & c. 54.	5		25 years.
(b) Reformatories. .	44 & 45 Vict., c. 29, .	3½ 3¾ 4	Not exceeding 30 years, 3½	20 years. 30 „ 35 „
(c) Industrial Schools, . .	48 Vict., c. 19 .	3½	35 „ 3	35 „
12. Dispensary houses, erection of,	42 & 43 Vict., c. 25, .	3¾		35 „
13. Lunatic asylums buildings, erection of, &c.	7 & 8 George 4, c. 33, 8 & 9 Vict., c. 107, 18 & 19 Vict., c. 109, 60 & 61 Vict., c. 77, and 56 & 57 Vict., c. 65.	3½		*50 years.
14. Housing of the working classes.	53 & 54 Vict., c. 70, .	3½ 3¾ 3½ 3¾ 3½	Not exceed-	30 years. 50 „ 40 „ 50 „

Purpose of Loan.	Authorising Acts.	Rate of Interest per Cent.	Maximum Period of Repayment.
Local Loans Fund.			
Loans not secured on Local Rates.			
1. Arterial drainage works,	26 & 27 Vict., c. 88, 28 & 29 Vict., c. 52, 37 & 38 Vict., c. 32, 43 & 44 Vict., c. 27.	4 during progress of works, subsequently 3½.	35 years. Compound sum (Principal, with interest during progress of works) repayable by annuity of £6 10s. per cent. for 22 years, or £5 per cent. for 35 years.
2. Maintenance of drainage works,	29 & 30 Vict., c. 49.	3	Various periods, not usually exceeding 18 years.
3. Railways and Tramways,	1 & 2 Wm. 4, c. 33, and Tramways Act, 1883.	4	35 years.
4. Reclamation of waste lands (see also Land Law Act, 1881).	1 & 2 Wm. 4, c. 33.	5	8 years from completion of works.
5. Loans to Pier Authorities created by Shannon Act, 1885.	Shannon Act, 1885,	Not less than 3½	30 years.
6. Glebe houses, erection of, and purchase of land, &c.	33 & 34 Vict., c. 112. 34 & 35 Vict., c. 100, and Expiring Laws Continuance Acts.	3½	35 years.
7. Land improvement preliminary expenses.	10 Vict., c. 32, s. 18,	—	—
8. Land improvement:— Loans to landlords— (a.) For subsoiling, trenching, irrigation, embanking, fencing, and reclamation of waste lands.	10 Vict., c. 32,	(about) 3½	22 years.
(b.) For farm buildings, houses, and offices, scutch mills, labourers' dwellings, and planting.	10 Vict., c. 32. 29 & 30 Vic., c. 40,	(about) 3½ 3½	22 „ 35 „
(c.) For labourers' cottages erected by order of Land Commission.	10 Vict., c. 32, s. 7, and Land Law Act, 1881, s. 19.	(about) 3½	22 „
9. National school teachers' residences, erection of.	38 & 39 Vict., c. 82.	3½	35 years.
10.* Dispensary houses, erection of,	42 & 43 Vict., c. 25,	3½	35 years.
11. Non-vested schools and training colleges, erection of.	47 & 48 Vict., c. 22,	3½	35 years.
12. Land Law Act, 1881, (a.) Loans to tenants for improvement of their holdings. (b.) Loans to Companies for reclamation of waste lands, &c.	44 & 45 Vict., c. 49, s. 31.	(about) 3½ 3½ 3½ 4 4½	22 years. 20 „ 30 „ 40 „ 50 „
13.* Housing of the working classes,	53 & 54 Vict., c. 70,	3½ 3½ 3½	30 years. 50 „ 50 „
Irish Church Fund.			
For erection of fishery piers and harbours.	46 & 47 Vict., c. 26,	3½	25 years.
Sea and Coast Fisheries Fund.			
To enable fishermen to purchase and repair boats, to supply fishing gear, &c.	47 & 48 Vict., c. 21. 54 & 55 Vict., c. 48.	2½	10 years.

* In cases where not secured on rates.

APPENDIX

TRAMWAYS AND PUBLIC COMPANIES (IRELAND)

Line.	County.	Length in Miles.	Order in Council. Date.	[illegible]	[illegible]	Area charged. [illegible]	Valuation.	[illegible]	[illegible]	[illegible]	[illegible]
1	2	3	4	5	6	7	8	9	10	11	12
1. [illegible] Valley.	Tyrone.	[illegible]	[illegible]	[illegible]	[illegible]	[illegible]	[illegible]	[illegible]	[illegible]	[illegible]	[illegible]
	[illegible]					[illegible]	[illegible]	+	–		[illegible]
2. Cavan and Leitrim.	Cavan.	[illegible]	[illegible]	[illegible]	[illegible]	[illegible]	[illegible]	[illegible]	[illegible]	[illegible]	[illegible]
	Leitrim.					[illegible]	[illegible]	[illegible]	[illegible]	[illegible]	[illegible]
3. West Clare.	Clare.	[illegible]	[illegible]	[illegible]	[illegible]	[illegible]	[illegible]	[illegible]	[illegible]	[illegible]	[illegible]
						[illegible]	[illegible]	[illegible]			
4. [illegible]	Antrim.	[illegible]	[illegible]	[illegible]	[illegible]	[illegible]	[illegible]	[illegible]	[illegible]	–	–
5. [illegible]	Cork.	[illegible]	[illegible]	[illegible]	[illegible]	[illegible]	[illegible]	[illegible]	[illegible]	[illegible]	[illegible]

1.

ACT, 1883, 46 & 47 VIC., CAP. 43.

Year.	First Half of Year.					Second Half of Year.					Annual Return.				
	Receipts.	Expenditure.	Balances. Credit.	Balances. Debit.	Treasury Contribution paid.	Receipts.	Expenditure.	Balances. Credit.	Balances. Debit.	Treasury Contribution paid.	Receipts.	Expenditure.	Balances. Credit.	Balances. Debit.	Treasury Contribution paid.
	£	£	£	£	£	£	£	£	£	£	£	£	£	£	£
[illegible]	—	—		—	—	[illegible]	[illegible]	[illegible]	—	[illegible]	[illegible]	[illegible]	[illegible]	—	[illegible]
[illegible]	[illegible]	[illegible]		[illegible]	[illegible]	[illegible]	[illegible]	[illegible]	—	[illegible]	[illegible]	[illegible]	—	[illegible]	[illegible]
[illegible]	[illegible]	[illegible]	—	[illegible]	[illegible]	[illegible]	[illegible]	[illegible]	—	[illegible]	[illegible]	[illegible]	—	[illegible]	[illegible]
[illegible]	[illegible]	[illegible]	—	[illegible]	[illegible]	[illegible]	[illegible]	—	[illegible]	[illegible]	[illegible]	[illegible]	—	[illegible]	[illegible]
[illegible]	[illegible]	[illegible]	—	[illegible]	[illegible]	[illegible]	[illegible]	[illegible]	—	[illegible]	[illegible]	[illegible]	—	[illegible]	[illegible]
[illegible]	[illegible]	[illegible]	—	[illegible]	[illegible]	[illegible]	[illegible]	[illegible]	—	[illegible]	[illegible]	[illegible]	[illegible]	—	[illegible]
[illegible]	[illegible]	[illegible]	—	[illegible]	[illegible]	[illegible]	[illegible]	[illegible]	—	[illegible]	[illegible]	[illegible]	[illegible]	—	[illegible]
[illegible]	[illegible]	[illegible]	—	[illegible]	[illegible]	[illegible]	[illegible]	[illegible]	—	[illegible]	[illegible]	[illegible]	—	[illegible]	[illegible]
[illegible]	[illegible]	[illegible]	—	[illegible]	[illegible]	[illegible]	[illegible]	[illegible]	—	[illegible]	[illegible]	[illegible]	—	[illegible]	[illegible]
[illegible]	[illegible]	[illegible]	—	[illegible]	[illegible]	[illegible]	[illegible]	[illegible]		[illegible]	[illegible]	[illegible]	—	[illegible]	[illegible]
[illegible]	[illegible]	[illegible]	—	[illegible]	[illegible]	[illegible]	[illegible]	[illegible]	—	[illegible]	[illegible]	[illegible]	[illegible]	—	[illegible]
[illegible]	[illegible]	[illegible]	—	[illegible]	[illegible]	—	—	—	—	—	—	—	—	—	—
[illegible]	—	—	—	—	—	—	—	—	—	[illegible]	—	—	—	—	[illegible]
[illegible]	[illegible]	[illegible]	—	[illegible]	[illegible]	[illegible]	[illegible]	[illegible]	—	[illegible]	[illegible]	[illegible]	[illegible]	—	[illegible]
[illegible]	[illegible]	[illegible]	—	[illegible]	[illegible]	[illegible]	[illegible]	—	[illegible]	[illegible]	[illegible]	[illegible]	—	[illegible]	[illegible]
[illegible]	[illegible]	[illegible]	—	[illegible]	[illegible]	[illegible]	[illegible]	—	[illegible]	[illegible]	[illegible]	[illegible]	—	[illegible]	[illegible]
[illegible]	[illegible]	[illegible]	—	[illegible]	[illegible]	[illegible]	[illegible]	—	[illegible]	[illegible]	[illegible]	[illegible]	—	[illegible]	[illegible]
[illegible]	[illegible]	[illegible]	—	[illegible]	[illegible]	[illegible]	[illegible]	—	[illegible]	[illegible]	[illegible]	[illegible]	—	[illegible]	[illegible]
[illegible]	[illegible]	[illegible]	—	[illegible]	[illegible]	[illegible]	[illegible]	[illegible]	—	[illegible]	[illegible]	[illegible]	[illegible]	—	[illegible]
[illegible]	[illegible]	[illegible]	[illegible]	—	[illegible]	[illegible]	[illegible]	[illegible]	—	[illegible]	[illegible]	[illegible]	[illegible]	—	[illegible]
[illegible]	[illegible]	[illegible]	[illegible]	—	[illegible]	[illegible]	[illegible]	[illegible]	—	[illegible]	[illegible]	[illegible]	[illegible]	—	[illegible]
[illegible]	[illegible]	[illegible]	[illegible]	—	[illegible]	[illegible]	[illegible]	[illegible]	—	[illegible]	[illegible]	[illegible]	[illegible]	—	[illegible]
[illegible]	[illegible]	[illegible]	—	[illegible]	[illegible]	[illegible]	[illegible]	[illegible]	—	[illegible]	[illegible]	[illegible]	[illegible]	—	[illegible]
[illegible]	[illegible]	[illegible]	[illegible]	—	[illegible]	—	—	—	—	—	—	—	—	—	—
[illegible]	—	—	—	—	—	[illegible]	[illegible]	[illegible]	—	[illegible]	[illegible]	[illegible]	[illegible]	—	[illegible]
[illegible]	[illegible]	[illegible]	—	[illegible]	[illegible]	[illegible]	[illegible]	[illegible]	—	[illegible]	[illegible]	[illegible]	[illegible]	—	[illegible]
[illegible]	[illegible]	[illegible]	—	[illegible]	[illegible]	[illegible]	[illegible]	[illegible]	—	[illegible]	[illegible]	[illegible]	[illegible]	—	[illegible]
[illegible]	[illegible]	[illegible]	—	[illegible]	[illegible]	[illegible]	[illegible]	[illegible]	—	[illegible]	[illegible]	[illegible]	[illegible]	—	[illegible]
[illegible]	[illegible]	[illegible]	—	[illegible]	[illegible]	[illegible]	[illegible]	[illegible]	—	[illegible]	[illegible]	[illegible]	[illegible]	—	[illegible]
[illegible]	[illegible]	[illegible]	—	[illegible]	[illegible]	[illegible]	[illegible]	[illegible]	—	[illegible]	[illegible]	[illegible]	[illegible]	—	[illegible]
[illegible]	[illegible]	[illegible]	[illegible]	—	[illegible]	[illegible]	[illegible]	[illegible]	—	[illegible]	[illegible]	[illegible]	[illegible]	—	[illegible]
[illegible]	[illegible]	[illegible]	[illegible]	—	[illegible]	[illegible]	[illegible]	[illegible]	—	[illegible]	[illegible]	[illegible]	[illegible]	—	[illegible]
[illegible]	[illegible]	[illegible]	[illegible]	—	[illegible]	[illegible]	[illegible]	[illegible]	—	[illegible]	[illegible]	[illegible]	[illegible]	—	[illegible]
[illegible]	[illegible]	[illegible]	[illegible]	—	[illegible]	[illegible]	[illegible]	[illegible]	—	[illegible]	[illegible]	[illegible]	[illegible]	—	[illegible]
[illegible]	[illegible]	[illegible]	—	[illegible]	[illegible]	[illegible]	[illegible]	[illegible]	—	[illegible]	[illegible]	[illegible]	[illegible]	—	[illegible]
[illegible]	[illegible]	[illegible]	[illegible]	—	[illegible]	—	—	—	—	—	—	—	—	—	—
[illegible] by Board of [illegible]															
[illegible]	[illegible]	[illegible]	[illegible]	—	[illegible]	[illegible]	[illegible]	[illegible]	—	[illegible]	[illegible]	[illegible]	[illegible]	—	[illegible]
[illegible]	[illegible]	[illegible]	[illegible]	—	[illegible]	[illegible]	[illegible]	[illegible]	—	[illegible]	[illegible]	[illegible]	[illegible]	—	[illegible]
[illegible]	[illegible]	[illegible]	[illegible]	—	[illegible]	[illegible]	[illegible]	[illegible]	—	[illegible]	[illegible]	[illegible]	[illegible]	—	[illegible]
[illegible]	[illegible]	[illegible]	[illegible]	—	[illegible]	[illegible]	[illegible]	[illegible]	—	[illegible]	[illegible]	[illegible]	[illegible]	—	[illegible]
[illegible]	[illegible]	[illegible]	[illegible]	—	[illegible]	[illegible]	[illegible]	[illegible]	—	[illegible]	[illegible]	[illegible]	[illegible]	—	[illegible]
[illegible]	[illegible]	[illegible]	[illegible]	—	[illegible]	[illegible]	[illegible]	[illegible]	—	[illegible]	[illegible]	[illegible]	[illegible]	—	[illegible]
[illegible]	[illegible]	[illegible]	[illegible]	—	[illegible]	—	—	—	—	—	—	—	—	—	—

APPENDIX

TRAMWAYS AND PUBLIC COMPANIES (IRELAND)

County.	[illegible]	Order in Council: Date.	Order in Council: [illegible]	Order in Council: Rate [illegible]	Area charged: Description.	Area charged: Valuation.	Proportion [illegible]	[illegible]	[illegible]	[illegible]
2.	3.	4.	5.	6.	7.	8.	9.	10.	11.	12.
			£			£		£	£	£
Cork,	[illegible]	[illegible]	[illegible]	[illegible]	[illegible]	[illegible]	[illegible]	[illegible]	[illegible]	[illegible]
[illegible]	[illegible]	[illegible]	[illegible]	[illegible]	[illegible]	[illegible]	Full amount.	[illegible]	[illegible]	[illegible]
[illegible]	[illegible]	[illegible]	[illegible]	[illegible]	[illegible]	[illegible]	Full amount.	[illegible]	[illegible]	[illegible]
Dublin,	[illegible]	[illegible]	[illegible]	[illegible]	[illegible]	[illegible]	[illegible]	[illegible]	[illegible]	[illegible]
Wicklow,					[illegible]	[illegible]	[illegible]			[illegible]

I.—*continued.*

Act, 1883, 46 & 47 Vic., cap. 43.

[illegible]	[illegible]					[illegible]					[illegible]			
[illegible]	[illegible]	[illegible]	[illegible]	[illegible]	[illegible]	[illegible]	[illegible]	[illegible]	[illegible]	[illegible]	[illegible]	[illegible]	[illegible]	[illegible]
[illegible]	[illegible]	[illegible]	[illegible]	[illegible]	[illegible]	[illegible]	[illegible]	[illegible]	[illegible]	[illegible]	[illegible]	[illegible]	[illegible]	[illegible]

APPENDIX

TRAMWAYS AND PUBLIC COMPANIES (IRELAND)

	County	Length in Miles	Order in Council: Date	Order in Council: [illegible]	Order in Council: [illegible]	Area charged: [illegible]	[illegible]	[illegible]	[illegible]	[illegible]	[illegible]
	1	2	3	4	5	6	7	8	9	10	11
[illegible]	Cork,	[illegible]	1st [illegible] 18[illegible]	[illegible]	[illegible]	[illegible]	[illegible]	[illegible]	[illegible]	[illegible]	[illegible]
[illegible]	Galway,	[illegible]	[illegible] July, 18[illegible]	[illegible]	[illegible]	[illegible]	[illegible]	[illegible]	[illegible]	[illegible]	[illegible]
[illegible]	[illegible]	[illegible]	[illegible]	[illegible]	[illegible]	[illegible]	[illegible]	[illegible]	[illegible]	[illegible]	[illegible]
[illegible]	[illegible]	[illegible]	[illegible]	[illegible]	[illegible]	[illegible]	[illegible]	[illegible]	[illegible]	[illegible]	[illegible]
[illegible]	Clare,	[illegible]	[illegible]	[illegible]	[illegible]	[illegible]	[illegible]	[illegible]	[illegible]	[illegible]	[illegible]
[illegible]	[illegible]	[illegible]	[illegible]	[illegible]	[illegible]	[illegible]	[illegible]	[illegible]	[illegible]	[illegible]	[illegible]
[illegible]	[illegible]	[illegible]	[illegible]	[illegible]	[illegible]	[illegible]	[illegible]	[illegible]	[illegible]	[illegible]	[illegible]

APPENDIX

TRAMWAYS AND PUBLIC COMPANIES (IRELAND)

County	[illegible]	Order in Council			Area charged		[illegible]	[illegible]	[illegible]	[illegible]
		Date	[illegible]	[illegible]	Description	Valuation				
[illegible]	[illegible]	[illegible]	[illegible]	[illegible]	[illegible]	[illegible]	[illegible]	[illegible]	[illegible]	[illegible]
Kerry	[illegible]	[illegible]	[illegible]	[illegible]	[illegible]	[illegible]	[illegible]	[illegible]	[illegible]	[illegible]
Kerry	[illegible]	[illegible]	[illegible]	[illegible]	[illegible]	[illegible]	[illegible]	[illegible]	[illegible]	[illegible]
Sligo	[illegible]	[illegible]	[illegible]	[illegible]	[illegible]	[illegible]	[illegible]	[illegible]	[illegible]	[illegible]
Mayo	[illegible]	[illegible]	[illegible]	[illegible]	[illegible]	[illegible]	[illegible]	[illegible]	[illegible]	[illegible]
[illegible]	[illegible]	[illegible]	[illegible]	[illegible]	[illegible]	[illegible]	[illegible]	[illegible]	[illegible]	[illegible]

www.ingramcontent.com/pod-product-compliance
Lightning Source LLC
Chambersburg PA
CBHW021948160426
43195CB00011B/1279

* 9 7 8 3 7 4 2 8 0 4 1 5 0 *